Copyright © 2020 by CF Web Voyager, LLC

All rights reserved.

No part of this publication may be reproduced, stored in a retrieval system, stored in a database and / or published in any form or by any means, electronic, mechanical, photocopying, recording or otherwise, without the prior written permission of the publisher.

www.exboyfriendrecovery.com
www.exboyfriend.com
www.ungettable.com

Ungettable

Becoming The Woman Every Man Wants

■

CHRIS SEITER

Contents

The Ungettable Girl **9**
The Results of The Ungettable **13**
Unrealistic Expectations, Momentum and Willpower **17**
The Holy Trinity Is The Weapon of The Ungettable **27**
Health **31**
Wealth **39**
Relationships **43**
Interconnection **47**
Looks vs. Personality **53**
Focusing On What You Can Control **57**
The Twelve **63**
Regret and the ideal self **115**
The 80/20 Rule **119**
Stop Putting Men On Pedestals **127**
Leverage **131**
From Men; The Perfect Woman **137**
Spinning Out of Control **147**
Avoiding The Downward Spiral **151**
Overcoming Irrational Thinking **153**
Mind Like Water **155**
Why We Procrastinate **159**
The Top Reasons People Aren't Ungettable **161**
How Do You Overcome Procrastination? **163**
The Struggle For Perfection **169**

Part One

The Ungettable Mindset

"Love and war are the same thing, and stratagems and policy are as allowable in the one as in the other."

-Miguel De Cervantes

One

The Ungettable Girl

We've been lied to.

That is a truth that almost no one realizes until it's too late.

We grew up in a society where our parents were always telling us that we could do anything we wanted.

Be anything we wanted to be.

They gave us participation trophies to make us feel included, but in the end, all they ended up doing was making us falsely believe that we are entitled to win.

Life, unfortunately, doesn't work that way, especially when it comes to relationships with men.

How often has a man told you that you weren't good enough, that you didn't have what it takes to make the relationship work?

"It's not you, it's me," they tell you as they concoct their seemingly selfless lie.

What they mean to say is, "It's you, not me."

Men can be cruel that way, but men are also prone to the fatal flaw that all human beings share.

Self-interest.

> *You see, the sooner you realize that what it all boils down to is the logic of "what's in it for me," the sooner their actions begin to make sense.*

Some of you may find this horrifying as you look back on your previous relationships with men, but I tell you this not to scare you but to help you understand.

In war, nothing is more significant than knowing and understanding your opponent.

And make no mistake about it, love is war.

Easy to begin, hard to stop.

But how does one win at love or war?

Simple, you need an edge.

Genghis Khan had the Mongol bow, he won.

The United States had the atomic bomb; they won.

But these are weapons of war.

What weapon is there in love?

Perhaps there is none greater for women than that of the Ungettable Girl.

The ultimate object of desire.

One that can never be reached but is always sought after.

And yet when asked directly about what this mythic woman is, most men can't describe the essence of what makes her special.

Perhaps this is a side effect of the fact that for every single person being "Ungettable" is different.

They say that beauty is in the eye of the beholder.

That's certainly true here.

But being "Ungettable" can't be summed up with a singular word.

It's a mistake most women make, especially when hearing about the concept for the first time.

Their mind jumps immediately to images of unobtainable beauty.

Supermodels in magazines.

But in my experience, supermodels in magazines aren't Ungettable.

They're just pretty.

And as you'll learn later in this book, being pretty can only get you so far.

So, how can we define the undefinable?

It's something I've struggled to explain to women for years, and I think it's because defining a concept like Ungettable is a little like trying to hit a moving target.

When you think you have a perfectly succinct definition, another aspect of the puzzle crops up to make you realize that you were wrong.

So, perhaps instead of giving you a traditional definition, it would be better to show you the results of what being Ungettable can do for you.

Two

The Results of The Ungettable

I find it's always best to tackle broad concepts like this with stories and analogies.

So, I ask you a straightforward question

Have you ever instantly clicked with someone during a date?

And I'm not talking about being on a date for a few hours and thinking to yourself,

"Wow, this person is fascinating."

I'm talking about instantly.

Within the first ten minutes, knowing deep down that this person gets you.

That feeling.

That calmness merely is touching the outskirts of what an Ungettable girl feels like to a man.

Often you'll hear men who are total players claim that they found "the one."

She's the type of girl that stops a man in his tracks, and there's no looking back.

I'll give you a real-life example.

If you didn't already know, I am a married man, and my wife has this "ungettable" quality.

But what I haven't talked a lot about is the exact thought process I had when I first laid eyes on her.

Our story is like so many others in the millennial age.

We met online.

Facebook, to be exact.

It was a few days after Christmas, and I happened to be randomly scrolling through my news feed when I happened across a video of this beautiful woman giving a present to a little girl.

My first thought was,

"That's the type of girl that I want to be with."

And to make a long story short, I was right.

I went out and married her.

Now, the story of how I got her isn't relevant right now.

The first thought I had when I saw her is.

You see, I knew immediately upon laying eyes on her, through a video on Facebook, that she was the type of woman I needed in my life.

I came to this conclusion without even talking to her once.

That is truly the essence of the ungettable quality.

Think of it like an invisible aura that surrounds "higher quality" women.

Often you'll hear sports announcers in baseball talking about the elusive "It" as in that player has "It."

When asked to quantify what "It" is, they can't give you a straight answer because the essence of "It" is impossible to quantify.

The ungettable quality or aura is a little like that, except over the decade I've been a dating and breakup coach, I've noticed specific patterns of the ungettable.

And that's what this book is about.

It's about me peeling back the layers so that you can identify these patterns and model your behavior after them.

By doing so, you'll notice a dramatic difference in how men treat you.

They'll start to respond to your texts with real depth.

They'll ask you out on dates.

Exes can come back and tell you that they've made a mistake.

The sky is the limit when you are "Ungettable."

But don't let the fact that I'm going to show you the patterns get to your head.

I've learned in my decade of research that there is a difference in the knowing and the doing.

Just because you understand something doesn't necessarily mean that you will execute it.

Also, there are genetic factors that come into play.

America was founded on the belief that all men are created equal, and while that's a beautiful sentiment, biology tells a different story.

Some people are given genetic advantages over others, which means that those few lucky people will have an easier time of becoming "ungettable."

But in the end, I've found that hard work beats talent when talent doesn't work hard.

So, my challenge to you as you read through this book is to work hard to model your dating life after the patterns I've worked so hard to discover.

Doing so could be the difference between failure and success.

However, you define that.

Three

Unrealistic Expectations, Momentum and Willpower

This entire book will tackle some profound concepts, the kind of ideas that can't be mastered in a few hours.

For some odd reason, this is a common misconception that I find people have.

They buy a self-help book, read it, get all fired up, and then do nothing.

The problem in my mind is unrealistic expectations.

I'm most known for my work helping men and women through breakups. I wouldn't be shocked if you heard about this very book through my breakup business.

Something fascinating happens when I work with these clients.

They almost always start off wanting me to help them get their exes back, and after a coaching session, they all tell me how excited they are to try out the new strategies that we have discussed.

I estimate only about half of them see those strategies through.

Why?

What is it that causes so many to deviate or not even try?

Is it laziness?

Is it something else?

Well, one thing I've learned is that passion alone isn't going to be enough.

What it all boils down to in the end is fear of failure and the negative consequences attached to it.

People often set entirely unrealistic expectations when they embark on a life-changing mission and make no mistake about it becoming ungettable is a lifelong pursuit.

I once watched this fascinating documentary called "The Barkley Marathons: The Race That Eats It's Young" that serves as a perfect allegory for unrealistic expectations.

It's considered to be the most challenging race in human history. In all, only 15 people have ever completed it.

For many, just completing one loop of this insane race is considered to be a lifelong achievement.

Here's how the race works.

Every year thousands of racers apply to race in "The Barkleys," but only 45 are chosen.

Entry into the race is very selective and requires a written essay and for you to bring a license plate from your home state.

What's fascinating is that many people outside the United States want to enter it and so you'll see people from France or England attempt the feat.

The race itself is held in the heart of the U.S. in Tenessee, and you're required to complete it in 60 hours.

So, if you go 100 miles in 60 hours, you will have completed the race.

It seems easy, right?

You're crazy if you think it is.

You aren't ever going in a straight line, and you're climbing hills and small mountains.

You have to contend with elements and go off the road.

Oh, and did I mention that the people who complete the race don't get any sleep.

Well, that's not entirely accurate.

One of the finishers got a total of one hour.

Imagine that for a moment, you are always walking and running for sixty hours straight.

No stopping.

Just pain.

It's not uncommon to have hallucinations due to sleep deprivation.

I'm telling you this not to show you how insane this race is but to show you how crazy the people are who embark on it.

Completing this thing takes extensive training and even a bit of luck.

If the weather is too hot or too cold, you're going to be in an unbelievable amount of pain.

Now, remember when I said that every year, only 45 athletes are allowed to compete?

Well, it turns out that the organizers of the event have an odd sense of humor.

After reading through thousands of qualifications, they purposefully pick someone who they know will fail.

Yep, it's an odd sense of humor indeed.

Now, I feel it's important to mention that technically speaking, there are no "unqualified" people who enter this race.

Every single person who applies has some skill in marathon racing, hike racing, tracking, etc.

But to master this race, you have to be good at everything.

In the documentary, the "human sacrifice" that the organizers decided to humble was this beefy army guy.

One look at the guy and you'd think to yourself,

"This is a man other men look up to."

He looked to be in great shape, had excellent navigation skills, and perhaps most importantly, he seemed very strong mentally.

And yet the organizers know exactly what type of person fails at this race, one who sets unrealistic expectations.

Remember, this is a race that almost no one ever completes.

This army guy went in thinking he would complete it.

After just a few hours, he folded.

He was the first to fold but was quickly joined by dozens of others.

Forty-five started the race, and after the first lap, only 19 were left.

What can this physical test of endurance teach us about life?

Well, I like to think of it as life personified.

Many years go by in this race, where no one ever completes it.

It tests every aspect of a human that you can think of, their ability to work with others, their ability to endure hardship and pain, how they feel, and how they act.

Every year the race changes to offer new challenges to those who have already competed in it.

So, how does one complete a race like this?

And what lesson can we take about "unrealistic expectations" from it?

The documentary I watched followed many racers in this hell on earth, but the one I gravitated most to was a guy by the name of John Fegyveresi.

Looking at him, you wouldn't expect much.

He's gaunt and wears these nerdy looking glasses.

Towards the end of the race, he was even moving like an old grandpa.

But somehow, he conquered this behemoth by himself. The odds were definitely against him, and yet he did it.

I think he may have the most mental courage I've ever seen in a human being.

He also had a lot of wisdom to pass on.

He tells this story about his father, a man he adored that had passed away a year earlier.

His father spent his entire life playing by society's rules.

You get up, work, put money away, and when you get to retirement, you visit all the places you've ever wanted to visit.

That's how life is supposed to work.

And that's what his father did.

He saved up his money and was ready to travel the world with his wife.

One year before he was ready for retirement, he passed away.

The grief shook John to his core.

To see his father die so close to his retirement flipped his worldview upside down.

Things aren't supposed to work that way.

Where is the payoff?

It isn't fair.

But rather than letting the experience send him down the spiral of despair, he used it as fuel to live in the moment.

He realized that a life that isn't fully lived isn't a life at all.

He entered this race to prove that he could do it.

Maybe he did it for his father.

Maybe he just wanted to exorcise his demons with life because whether you realize it or not, causality isn't fair.

Good people die every day, and bad people go on living.

Where is the fairness there?

John just decided to show that an average guy can complete the hardest race in the world.

He did it.

But it wasn't easy.

He recorded the slowest time ever in Barkley History for a finisher, but he did finish.

He got zero hours of sleep.

He was hallucinating, and yet he held on.

What can John teach us about being ungettable?

Well, he went into the Barkleys with realistic expectations. He knew completing the race was unlikely and would take something deep inside.

He knew he would be in extreme pain.

His feet would be riddled with so many blisters that he'd wonder if he would be able to go on.

He'd be sleep deprived.

He'd hallucinate.

He'd cry.

He'd want to quit.

He'd limp into the finish line.

He knew it would be the most painful experience of his life, and he prepared for it mentally.

He pushed through the sleep deprivation.

He recognized the hallucinations for that they were, distractions.

He'd allow himself to cry and then get up and move on.

UNREALISTIC EXPECTATIONS, MOMENTUM AND WILLPOWER

He'd never quit even when he knew it was what his body wanted more than anything.

Limping wouldn't matter.

He had the essential things needed to finish an unfinishable race, momentum, and willpower.

If you want to be ungettable, you are going to need those two things.

So many people never complete their goals because they set unrealistic expectations and never create the momentum needed to succeed.

> *Action is almost always better than inaction.*

Sometimes all you need to accomplish something in life is to get started and stay started.

Momentum can carry you to the end, but willpower will ensure that the momentum continues.

That's what John understood.

Why do you think he refused to sleep?

He knew if he did, he'd quit.

He'd drift away into the land of dreams and never want to leave.

I guarantee you he wanted nothing more than to lay his head down and rest.

But his willpower wouldn't let him.

He knew that if he did, it would be all over, and once you stop the momentum, that's it.

John had one more thing to say about his experience that I want to leave you within this chapter.

He said that everyone could use a little pain in their lives because it makes you appreciate the quiet moments that much more.

The path to being ungettable may be painful.

You may not like it.

But if you see it through to the end, I guarantee you'll appreciate it.

Part Two
The Holy Trinity

"The best and safest thing is to keep a balance in your life, acknowledge the great powers around us and in us. If you can do that, and live that way, you are really a wise man."

-Euripides

Four

The Holy Trinity is The Weapon of The Ungettable

Entropy is a universal force acting during every moment of our existence.

Some scientists believe that life emerged as a feature of the increasing entropy of the universe.

Now, while we can debate the philosophical and religious consequences of that statement for hours, one thing I think we can all agree on is that the law of entropy exists.

I'll give you an example.

Let's say that you go to the beach and decide that you want to build a sandcastle.

You spend hours building it, and when it's finally complete, you are very impressed with your work.

But it's time to go home.

You spent all day building your castle, and it's almost dark.

The question here is, does your castle still stand when you come back the next day?

Definitely not.

But why?

Well, you have forces such as the wind and the tide to take into account. At some point during the night, they will conquer your castle.

This is entropy at work.

It turns order into chaos because chaos is the natural state of the universe.

What makes human beings so special is that we are the only known intelligent life to create order out of chaos.

It's what makes us great.

But that doesn't mean that chaos is gone.

On the contrary, chaos is always hanging over our heads like the Sword of Damocles.

Consider for a moment, my job.

I teach women to take a chaotic situation, where a guy doesn't like them and create order, where a guy does fall for them.

But this can't be done without first creating order in your own life.

That's where the holy trinity comes into play.

Now, when I first introduce this concept to women, they always think I'm talking about something biblical.

That's not what the concept is.

However, I find that women who treat it with religious reverence tend to have better results with men.

Perhaps that's because they create an ideal balance in their own lives.

So, what is it?

I think we can all agree that human life can't be distilled down into simplistic categories.

However, if we were to distill it down into the three most important categories, what would they be?

Most likely, they'd be health, wealth, and relationships.

Hence the name, holy trinity.

If you want to become ungettable, you must first find balance in your own life, and that starts with looking at these three aspects of your life and maximizing them.

Create order out of the chaos.

Five

Health

Most of the people I work with who struggle with the health aspect of the holy trinity are going through breakups.

Now, a funny thing happens when people go through breakups.

They let themselves go.

Physically and mentally.

Don't discount that mental portion of the equation just because you can't see the impact physically.

For someone going through a breakup, the descent into chaos often happens through the health pillar.

As they are consumed with thoughts of the breakup, they lose their drive to eat food, which negatively impacts health.

Some have the opposite effect.

They derive pleasure from eating food and overeat.

Again, another negative hit to health.

Some continue to take care of their bodies, but the stress of the breakup manifests itself in strange ways.

Losing hair, for example.

In 1961, Roger Maris captivated the world as he launched an assault on

Babe Ruth's most famous record.

60 home runs.

It was thought that the mark would stand forever, and yet here was Roger Maris, who was closing in quickly.

But the sportswriters were infamous for being hard on him.

They didn't want to see their precious idol in Ruth dethroned by the lowly Maris.

As the stakes were raised, Maris started losing his hair from the stress.

A mental pressure that manifested physically.

He broke the record, by the way, 61 home runs.

Here's my point.

Health is a pillar that can impact you in a variety of ways.

So, how can you balance out the health portion of your life?

Well, I find it's essential to divide health up into two main categories.

1. Physical Manifestations

2. Emotional Manifestations

Let's talk about taking the negative physical manifestations and improving them.

IMPROVING PHYSICAL MANIFESTATIONS

This might be the most challenging section of the entire book because we are going to be opening up and exploring some of the most challenging aspects of your life, things like your weight or physical insecurities.

However, I feel it's only fair that if I'm asking you to open up to me that I first open up to you by telling you my biggest physical insecurity.

An eye for an eye, so to speak.

Growing up, I always struggled with the fact that I had an imperfection.

I felt my face was handsome.

I was comfortable with my body.

But the one flaw was the fact that I had this tiny little mole on my neck.

Bear in mind, most people didn't even notice it, but I sure did.

I was so embarrassed about it that I wore a hoody to school every single day during the sixth grade because I learned that was the best way to cover it up.

I distinctly remember being asked during the heat of summer by my classmates why I was wearing a hoody.

"It's comfortable," I would lie.

The real reason was to hide the shame of my mole.

Soon as I hit high school, I found a much less obvious way to cover it.

Tight under armour shirts were vital.

Failing that, wearing a white undershirt underneath another shirt did the trick.

That's why if you look at any photos of me from high school, I probably am wearing one of those two things.

It wasn't for looks.

But even that wasn't enough to cover it all the time. Soon I developed this ridiculous tick where I would walk around with my shoulders higher than usual.

My thinking was that the shirts wouldn't fall, and I would be able to retain my ideal image.

Of course, throughout a day, I would find that my solution was imperfect, so I'd always have to adjust my shirt to move it up, and here, another tick was born.

I bet if you watch some of my earliest YouTube videos, you can find this tick.

Shoulders high.

Adjust the shirt.

Rinse and repeat.

For almost fifteen years, I lived with this embarrassment.

It sounds ridiculous now that I'm putting it on paper for the world to see, but this was something I was deathly afraid of mentioning in public.

No one knew.

It became exceptionally debilitating as I entered the dating scene for the first time.

I became extra self-conscious of this imperfection and allowed it to control me.

Instead of focusing on entertaining girls on dates, all I cared about was making sure they couldn't see my mole.

I remember as I met my wife for the very first time, I thought to myself,

"God, she's so perfect. If I show her my imperfection, she'll be disgusted by me, and things will fall apart."

She doesn't even know this, but I remember the very first time she tried to video chat with me. I didn't pick up.

I got the video chat invite, but I wasn't wearing the right clothes to cover up.

So, I scrambled across my room to find the right type of shirt before I called her back.

Yes, my physical imperfection became quite a hindrance. Any time things went wrong on a date, it was the first thing I'd blame.

Instead of realizing that maybe I wasn't a fit for the girl it'd always be,

HEALTH 35

"Damn this mole. It's always the reason women won't fall for me."

The ironic part was that it was so small no one probably even noticed, but you couldn't tell that to me because I had made it so big in my head that it became this fatal flaw that held me back.

I think everyone has these fatal flaws that hold them back in life when it comes to physical manifestations.

The important thing that you need to remember is that there are some physical manifestations that you can control and others you can't.

Here are some of the most common physical manifestations you usually have some measure of control over.

Your weight (Working out)

Your clothes (Buying new clothes)

Your hair (Haircuts, new hairstyles)

Your teeth (brushing your teeth)

Your hygiene (do I have to explain this one?)

I find that the ungettable has a handle over the aspects of physical beauty that they can control.

However, where they shine is in how they handle the aspects they can't control.

My opening up to you about my insecurity was a genetic aspect that I had no control over.

So, how do you master the physical insecurities of your life that you have no control over?

In my opinion, there is only one way.

The paradigm shift.

The reason I can talk about my insecurity is that I had a massive paradigm shift a few years ago.

You see, if you distill my insecurity down to its most basic form, it's really about not feeling good enough.

Because I had this debilitating thought about my looks, I created this narrative that I kept feeding to myself.

"My mole makes me not good enough."

"No one can love me because I look like this."

It wasn't until I was with my wife, and I told her about my fears that she said to me that my little mole was one of the things she loved about me.

I couldn't believe my ears.

She explained to me that it made me cute.

Though I'm pretty sure she called it a beauty mark, which makes it sound a lot more dignified.

Throughout my entire life, I had never once considered that there could be people out there that would fall in love with beauty marks.

This paradigm shift was revolutionary to me.

And it's something I notice the ungettable do so well. You see, they live life without needing validation from others.

They inherently understand what took me so long to realize.

People come in all shapes and sizes, and for every insecurity that those shapes and sizes create, there are people out there that will love you for it.

But physical insecurities aren't the only manifestations of health that the holy trinity covers.

We also have emotional manifestations.

IMPROVING EMOTIONAL MANIFESTATIONS

Emotional manifestations of health are most common for people who have debilitating beliefs about themselves.

The story I told about myself was a perfect example of this. I took a physical insecurity about myself and made it worse because my mind created this false narrative.

"You aren't good enough."

"You're ugly."

"No one will ever love you."

These were all thoughts that I had throughout my life, and the ironic part was that my conscious was proven to be a liar the second my wife told me she loved my insecurity.

This is what created a paradigm shift for me, and I've already alluded to the fact that if you can't overcome these emotional insecurities about yourself, it's going to take a paradigm shift to do so.

I hope that I can stir the paradigm shift for you with this book.

We already know that the ungettable are these seemingly perfect creatures with the ability to wrap men around their fingers.

However, it's essential to keep in mind that they didn't always start out that way.

It's just that they look at the world in a different way than you or I.

Instead of thinking, "I'm not good enough."

They think, "The world isn't good enough for me."

They are supremely confident, and it seeps into almost all the areas of their lives.

Now, emotional insecurities aren't easy to cure.

Having me say,

"Feel better and be ungettable."

Isn't going to do anything.

But I'd like to submit the fact that the ungettable understands more than anyone.

Time is your most valuable resource.

Not money, though even I debate with myself about that one sometimes. But in the end, there are thousands of ways to make money for yourself.

Time is the only thing once spent, that you can't get back.

The scary part.

None of us knows how much time we have in our "bank accounts."

Most people, when confronted with this fact, find ways to push it away or compartmentalize it, so they don't have to think about it.

It is a morbid fact.

We will all die, and none of us knows when.

In my opinion, there are two types of people.

Those who confront this fact and ensure they are spending their time wisely.

And those who run from this fact and continue to be sheep – slaving away for a world that doesn't care about them.

Which category do you think an ungettable falls into?

Instead of letting the world and its people control them, they master their fate and live life on their terms.

This is the paradigm shift that took me thirty years to fully grasp.

My problems and insecurities are small and not worth worrying about in the grand scheme of things.

I have this touchstone I continuously come back to.

Whenever I get insecure about something I always think,

"Will I even care about this if I'm on my deathbed?"

If my answer is yes, then I know it's probably worth worrying about.

However, if my answer is no, then I know not even to let it bother me.

The world is full of people worrying and obsessing over small problems.

Don't let the fear control you.

You control the fear.

Six

Wealth

Most people, when thinking about wealth, jump immediately to monetary terms.

How much money do I have?

But I think it's short-sighted to view wealth in this way. Sure, wealth and money go hand in hand, but there are other areas of life where wealth can be experienced.

To name a few,

- Money
- Possessions
- Personal Property
- Career
- Spiritual Wealth
- Social Capital
- Education

Years ago, I was once asked by a client if I could describe the holy trinity better for her.

After taking some time to consider, the analogy I decided upon was mind, body, and soul.

- The Body (Health)
- The Mind (Wealth)
- The Soul (Relationships)

Most of the people I work with make the mistake of looking at wealth in entirely monetary terms and forget to cultivate their minds.

I'd argue that cultivating your mind might be even more important than improving your body.

Why?

Well, to answer that, we are going to have to get philosophical and attempt to answer the most unanswerable question there is.

What is the meaning of life?

Ask a thousand different philosophers the question, and you'll probably get a thousand different answers.

And while this philosopher doesn't have all the answers, I do have a hypothesis on what I believe the meaning of life is.

Meaning can be found in three different activities.

1. Communication
2. Understanding
3. Service

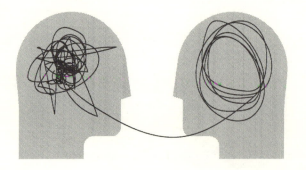

Let's look at communication first. We are, by nature, isolated creatures, and it appears that some of our most meaningful moments are derived when connecting with others, lovers, friendships, family.

You take these three pillars of communication away from a human, and most likely, you'll find a floundering existence.

Let's move on and talk about understanding next.

Meaning is derived here when we correct confusion or puzzlement about our understanding of the world.

It's why pieces of art, like novels or books, speak to us.

The good ones teach us something about the human condition. The bad ones typically don't.

Often you'll find humans are captivated with learning. This is why the creation of the internet is so fascinating and addicting.

If you think about it, it is the most extensive library in the world.

It is merely a place where we can go to learn something.

For some, it's experiencing life through others' lives (watching YouTube videos.)

For others, it's scanning the internet to learn about why their relationships never work out.

But in the end, it's always about cultivating your knowledge and helping you derive meaning in your life.

Finally, we have service.

One of the most meaningful things we can do is to serve other people.

To try to improve their lives by either alleviating their suffering or generating new sources of pleasure.

Most of you will jump to images of nurses or doctors, but you can also include people who write songs, film movies and write books in this category as well.

That's what this whole book is about if you think about it.

I'm trying to show you how to become ungettable, which will ideally alleviate suffering in your life.

But how does wealth fit into this idea?

My challenge for you at the beginning of this chapter was to try to look past superficial ideas like money and career when viewing this area of your life.

The pattern I notice for the ungettable in the wealth section of the holy trinity is that they are excellent at maxing out the meaning of their life.

They don't just look and feel great (health.)

They also work on understanding the world (wealth.)

They cultivate their minds to be the very best versions of themselves.

They seek to be more and are never satisfied.

Seven

Relationships

No great achievement is ever done alone.

This is something that took me years to realize.

Eventually, you are going to have to trust and rely upon other human beings.

The relationships portion of the holy trinity is perhaps the most straightforward ideal.

> *Your goal here is to cultivate the relationships in your life so that you are surrounding yourself with the best minds available.*

You've heard that old phrase that you are who you surround yourself with.

I've found that there is a lot of wisdom to be had from that statement.

Whoever you choose to surround yourself with will have this impact on your core values and your station in life.

I'll give you a direct example.

Let's say that you've surrounded yourself with a group of friends who do illegal things.

Chances are, at some point, that you are going to have a brush with the law yourself.

But let's take a break from this track and talk about the misconception that most women have about the relationships portion of the holy trinity.

Most women who aren't ungettable take this view that relationships are only supposed to be their lovers.

While they do technically fall into the "relationship" portion of the holy trinity, an ungettable girl understands that relationships are so much more than that.

- Friends
- Family
- Teachers
- Work Colleagues
- Counselors
- Therapists
- Clergy
- Pets

The ungettable has this knack for not hyper-focusing on just one single tribe of relationships.

Instead, they spread the love around to all tribes.

They have great relationships with their parents, friends, work colleagues, and even in some cases, pets.

Now, you may be sitting there and thinking,

"Wow, that seems easy."

That's probably because I haven't told you the hard part yet. They are incredibly methodical about who they surround themselves with.

If they deem they aren't getting anything positive out of a particular relationship, they end the relationship.

Most people are too scared to do this.

They think it's rude and that you should never treat anyone poorly, but I'm not sure I agree with that.

Sure, I don't think you should treat a friend poorly.

However, I also don't think you should walk around chained by what society thinks is right.

Everyone has that friend who only cares about themselves. Let's say you help them regularly when they have a problem, but you don't get anything in return.

Your conversations with them are one-sided, and pretty soon, you realize that the only time they ever talk to you is when they have a problem.

Does this sound like a good friend?

The difference between the ungettable and us is the fact that the ungettable isn't afraid to cut ties with a person like that.

A friendship should be a give and take relationship.

You should give your time and energy but so should they.

If you don't see the same level of dedication, then it might be time to look for a better friend.

The same can be said about the relationship with your significant others.

If you look back on your relationship and realize it was completely one-sided, then you have a problem.

Eight

Interconnection

This chapter may be the entire reason I wrote about the holy trinity.

If you didn't already know, I deal with a lot of clients who are going through breakups.

Besides telling them that they need to be ungettable and doing my best to explain what that is, I introduce them to the concept of the holy trinity.

But most of them fail to see the truth of how it works.

Now, I use the breakup example because it's highly related to the idea of interconnection.

There are three main areas of the holy trinity that we've talked about so far.

- Health
- Wealth
- Relationships

If you haven't already realized, the goal for an ungettable girl is to take those three areas and balance them.

To max out their health, their wealth, and their relationships.

What I haven't told you is that all of them are interconnected.

What impacts one area positively will also have a positive effect on the other areas.

Of course, there are two sides to every coin, and what impacts one negatively can also harm the other areas.

Let's take my most typical client as an example.

My most typical client is reeling from a breakup, which means their "relationships" portion of the holy trinity has taken a negative hit.

Of course, when you go through a breakup, you get all kinds of physical ailments.

- Sadness
- Depression
- Anger

Many women have many ways of coping with these feelings.

Some will take their problems head-on, but most will find ways to avoid or feel sorry for themselves.

As a result, their "health" takes a hit.

Maybe they are like me; they eat their feelings away.

Honestly, I'm not afraid to admit this.

A few years ago, I went through a difficult time in my online business.

Rather than facing the problem head-on, I did what I thought would make me feel better.

I ate everything that I've always wanted to eat.

The results were pretty clear.

I gained twenty pounds.

Here we have an example of "wealth" affecting "health."

But let's get back to our original example.

As "health" takes a hit, you become distracted or fall deeper into that depression quicksand, and you stop doing the best job you possibly can at work.

The result here is pretty clear.

You get yelled at by your boss, which makes you feel even worse and deeper you fall into the depression which you've grown so accustomed to.

Pretty soon, you hate your job, you are cluster eating, and as a result, your friends begin not to want to hang out with you.

All this from a simple breakup.

The holy trinity is interconnected.

Every negative has a deeper meaning than you realize. Of course, the opposite is also true.

Every positive can thunder exponentially across the holy trinity.

What makes ungettable girls so unique is that they understand this intricate balance and are always working to balance their lives.

But how should they do that in the breakup example above?

Well, when your relationship category takes a hit, contrary to popular belief, the last thing you should do is try to repair the relationship aspect of the holy trinity.

Instead, seek to improve seemingly unrelated aspects of your life.

Go all-in on health.

Go all-in on wealth.

When you start seeing positive changes there, you'll notice positive changes in the relationship aspect.

I have seen this concept work hundreds of times.

Trust in the interconnection of the holy trinity.

Part Three
The Book or The Cover?

"What matters more, the book or the cover?"

-CHRIS SEITER

Nine

Looks vs. Personality

Here's a question for the ages.

What matters more to men.

Looks or personality?

At the beginning of this book, I made an interesting statement.

> *"In my experience supermodels on magazines aren't Ungettable. They're just pretty."*

What I seem to mention here is that "looks" are overrated, and for the most part, I agree with that sentiment, but there are a few important points I'd like to touch on.

We live in a politically correct culture.

Everyone is afraid to rock the boat and stomp on politically correct beliefs.

I feel that this kind of thinking limits reality and prevents us from having a conversation that could change your life.

After all, if you have something important to say, you can't expect everyone to like it.

So, here's my hot take for the book.

Looks do matter.

Anyone who tells you otherwise is lying to you or afraid to hurt your feelings.

But not me.

My job is to make sure that you are ungettable, and if you want to obtain that status, then looks are a part of the equation.

There is no way around that fact.

But here's the part that most pretty girls forget.

It's not just about looking your best to a member of the opposite sex.

You need to have real depth to your personality.

I think there is an argument that can be made that hinges on the fact that the more "deep" you seem to a man, the more likely they are to stay with you.

The best analogy I have come up with to describe this process is that of the book versus the cover.

Reading is becoming a lost art, and that saddens me because it's one of the most effective ways that you can cultivate your knowledge of what it means to be human.

Sure, we can go to YouTube and watch a video on the meaning of life, but that's not quite the same as experiencing it through reading a book.

It's just more powerful.

Anyways, one of the most famous sayings of all time has to be not to judge a book by its cover.

And yet how often does someone go into a bookstore and do just that?

As if the cover tells the whole story to the experience of the story.

Generally, in fiction, the cover of a book is a snapshot of one singular moment in the book.

But should we make an entire book purchase based on a snapshot in time?

Maybe the moment looks cool, but the story is awful.

The truth is that the cover of a book is what grabs a buyer's attention and maybe even gets them to make a purchase, but the story of the book is what makes them rabid fans.

We can even distill this concept down to trailers for movies.

Sure, if a trailer looks fantastic, it makes you want to see the movie.

However, the trailer doesn't guarantee the movie is good.

In the end, the depth of the story always wins out. It's what makes people become lifelong fans.

And now we come full circle to looks versus personality.

In a perfect world, you'd be perfection personified in both beauty and personality, but how often do we live in an ideal society?

The saddest fact of the whole condition of our race is how superficial we have become.

If I lined one hundred women up and asked them what they would want more of, I would probably get one hundred answers stating the brilliance of beauty.

What all the "beautiful" people come to learn is that beauty alone doesn't equate to happiness.

Men cheat on and leave beautiful women just as much as average-looking women.

Beauty is overrated.

It's not what creates a lifelong commitment if that's what you want.

Think about that statement for a moment.

We all share the same destination.

None of us likes to think about that destination because it's scary and a bit morbid, but it doesn't make it any less real.

The closer we all get to death, we wrinkle, limp, and die.

We become weak, and by no definition, does this process make us look more beautiful.

From the moment we hit the peak of our lives, our cells are in a constant state of aging.

Beauty is fleeting.

Maybe that's the very reason everyone seems so obsessed with it.

What the ungettable realizes is that beauty alone won't capture the imagination of men.

It takes something more.

And that's really what this whole book is about.

Showing you what that is.

Ten

Focusing on What You Can Control

The human condition is one racked with worry and stress over things you can't control.

How often throughout a day do you worry about something you have no control over?

If you're anything like me, then it's probably a lot.

> *Focus on what you can control, leave what you can't.*

One can make an argument that those words are among the most important in the entire book.

And yet, it's easier said than done.

In chapter three, I opened up and told a very personal story to you.

I obsessed about a hardly noticeable physical imperfection for most of my young adult life.

It wouldn't be a stretch to say that it controlled me.

My thoughts fears and hopes often hinged upon how self-conscious I became during dates just because I thought I wasn't good enough.

Perhaps the most ironic part about the whole thing was the fact that I had no control over my genetics.

My fate was already decided for me at birth.

And yet, my obsession continued. It wasn't until I heard from someone that one of the reasons she fell in love with me was because of my physical imperfection that my paradigm shifted.

It was as if my mind had never even considered this outcome, and it became clear to me that life is wasted worrying about things you have no control over.

I wrote this book for women, and I know the pressure for them to "look perfect" is so much higher than it was for me, so I'm not going to pretend I understand every thought or fear you have about the way you look.

What I will say, though, is that if you spend time worrying about something you have no control over, you'll miss out on the opportunities to improve the aspects you do have control over.

This is a common mistake that business owners make.

They get tunnel vision and focus on improving one specific aspect of their business that they have no real control over, and as a result, everything else falls apart.

Instead, what the smart owners do is focus on all the aspects they do have control over and incrementally improve them.

That "incremental" improvement is the critical point to make here.

In business, there is always this insane pressure to create immense growth.

Most business owners would be tickled to death if they could grow their business by 100%.

And yet the biggest mistake I see these business owners make is focusing on growing one area of the business by 100%.

Instead, what they should be doing is picking ten areas of their business and growing it by 10%.

It's a different method with the same result.

It's a lot easier to improve something by 10% than it is to grow something by 100%.

I want you to think of your life in this way.

Instead of improving one area of your life dramatically that you have no control over pick ten areas and incrementally improve them.

The holy trinity comes into play here.

While there are generally only three main categories that it covers, it's important to remember that each "main category" has a bunch of little subcategories.

So, while health is a big category remember that it also includes concepts like

- Your weight (Working out)
- Your clothes (Buying new clothes)
- Your hair (Haircuts, new hairstyles)
- Your teeth (brushing your teeth)
- Emotional Mindset (growing confidence)

If you just incrementally "improve" each one of those areas, you'll notice your whole life gets an upgrade.

Part Four
The Qualities of The Ungettable

"Victorious warriors win first and then go to war, while defeated warriors go to war first and then seek to win."

-Sun Tzu

Eleven

The Twelve

Earlier in this book, I stated that defining what the ungettable quality is can be difficult.

Every one of us has our idea of what that looks like.

However, when you've been doing this for as long as I have, you begin to notice specific trends and patterns develop.

I'm a big subscriber to the Socratic method.

Essentially it's this framework to help you arrive at a truth by continually challenging your assumptions.

Think of it as the original scientific method before that was a thing.

I started my career helping people who were going through breakups.

Many of you who are reading this book are probably going through a break-up and are even trying to win your ex back.

After all, that's what most people who are going through a breakup want at one point.

The Socratic method becomes handy when you are responsible for putting together a professional game plan to do just that.

You come into the process, holding what you believe is a universal truth about what is going on in an exes mind only to be proved entirely wrong.

I learned early on that most of my peers ignored the truth in favor of promoting the fancy new shiny item even if it wasn't going to help.

For some reason, people believe the sexy buzzword products will help them when what they need is a Socratic approach to their situation.

They need someone who is continually testing and proving their previous hypotheses wrong.

Maybe it's impossible to arrive at the truth.

However, if you are dogged in your pursuit of learning what is considered "true," then with each correction, you'll get closer to perfection.

I've been doing that with the ungettable for close to ten years and have noticed that almost every "ungettable person" has exhibited twelve patterns.

Not every single one displays all twelve patterns, but for the most part, they are balanced in their seduction.

And make no mistake about it.

"The twelve" are an entryway into seducing everyone they interact with.

QUALITY #1 • THE DAYDREAM QUALITY

Did you know that there is a relationship between daydreaming and brain development?

Scientists have grown so curious about this link that some have ventured to claim that the more you daydream, the more intelligent you may be.

I think daydreaming gets a bad rap.

When I was in preschool, I was sent home with a unique report card.

One column contained my grades.

The other contained an attitude "grade."

Even though my grades were excellent, I always got points taken off because of my attitude.

Teachers would say things like.

"Chris gets good grades, but his mind always seems to wander."

"He's with us, but not really with us."

"Chris always seems to want to turn everything into a game."

Mostly I was being scolded for how I arrived at my good grades.

My mind worked a bit differently than everyone else, but because it wasn't "normal," it was looked at as a bad thing.

Now that I am a parent myself, I see a lot of this in my daughter.

She plays games by making up these fantastical scenarios, and it's a beautiful thing to watch.

Her mind works in a similar way to mine. My wife gets scared that she is falling behind in some of the "socially acceptable" forms.

But I'm always quick to point out how far ahead she is in all the other areas.

> Our ability to dream is powerful, and I think it should be encouraged.

But how does this all connect to the daydream quality of the ungettable?

Think back to your first serious relationship.

Everything is always so awkward.

You don't know what to say.

You don't know what to do and always second guess yourself spending hours dissecting every detail, every text.

It's a glorious mess.

I was always lost in the daydream of what could be as opposed to what was.

The most exciting part of my first crush were the quiet moments where I'd daydream about what life would look like if I could win this girl's heart.

Failure was met with heartache, and when I finally did succeed, the dreams always became bigger.

At first, the daydreams would start simple.

Could I get my first girlfriend?

What would that look like?

And then I got one.

Next, it became about kissing her for the first time and my goodness, what an awkward experience that was.

Soon, it became about taking her on an extended date.

Then I did that.

When each daydream met reality, the new fantasy would be bigger until I was rooted in the foundation of this relationship.

As I got older, I learned the sting that my fantasies and realities were often far different.

I think this is what separates the ungettable from the rest of us.

They understand how to use daydreams to seduce.

And they use a particular tactic.

> *They identify a person's most significant unmet need and fulfill it in a way that it's never been fulfilled before.*

Mainly they ensure that reality far exceeds fantasy.

It's not an easy thing to do because we are often a victim of our self-interest.

Each of us wants something from the world.

Some people may want a better job.

Others may want an ex back.

Then you'll have people who are obsessed with popularity.

But what I think everyone forgets is that there is a fundamental law that needs to be met if you want to achieve something.

You must first give something up to get what you want.

For a better job, you have to earn a promotion.

To get an ex back, you'll have to have a smart plan.

Want to get popular? Well, you'll need an audience. Want to get an audience? You'll have to do something noteworthy.

The list goes on and on forever.

But the law always remains the same.

Be willing to sacrifice and give something up to get what you want.

We often walk through our lives, thinking only about ourselves, but what the ungettable can do is view the world beyond their own selfish needs.

They'll look and identify the needs of others to seduce them.

How do they do this?

They have more productive conversations than the average person.

Instead of making the conversation about themselves, they listen and ask questions in a very pointed way to find out what a person's biggest frustrations in life are.

What they are doing is a very delicate dance where they are learning about you and determining what forces in your life drive you forward.

Slowly they begin to notice what your most significant unmet needs are, and they find ways to fulfill those needs.

So, here's my question for you. How often have you done this?

QUALITY #2 • THE POPULARITY QUALITY

I want to make one thing very clear.

Popularity is not a guarantee of quality.

However, it is undeniable that there is something about being popular that attracts us.

Take a look at how we worship celebrities or public figures.

But what is it about them that we are drawn to?

Their ability to act or sing?

Maybe.

Their status in life?

Potentially.

How much money they have?

Definitely.

Here's my hypothesis.

> *The popular are worshiped because they are the ultimate alphas of our race.*

They contain traits or characteristics that we wish we all had.

Think about it for a moment.

They usually only let beautiful people be actors.

Singers can charm the devil with their voices.

Politicians, for all their faults, have the power we desperately envy.

Billionaires have money.

You get the picture.

If there's one thing I'll say about the ungettable, it's that they are almost always popular.

They are loved among friends and family, sure.

But that's not how I'm defining popularity in this case.

The ungettable ooze desirable characteristics and gain status for those characteristics.

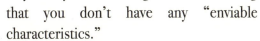

Don't let this fact intimidate you if you're reading this and thinking that you don't have any "enviable characteristics."

You do, you just haven't found your niche yet.

They say that to master a skill truly, you must meet a 10,000-hour requirement first.

In other words, you need to spend 10,000 hours learning and practicing everything you possibly can to master that particular skill.

Only then can you be considered an expert or master.

Assuming you spend one hour a day "mastering" your skill, it would take you approximately 27 years before you could be considered a master.

This is why we worship actors and singers.

They've spent countless hours honing and perfecting a skill that hardly anyone ever tries in their lives.

As a society, we recognize and appreciate that.

Here's my question for you.

What have you been spending your time doing?

Are you mastering a skill that will yield the popularity you need?

I'm asking you this seriously.

If you want to be popular, you have to create an unfair advantage for yourself.

A reason that others will be drawn to you.

Oh, and perhaps I should mention that this skill needs to improve the lives of others in some way because the more of an impact you can make on others, the more popular you will become.

Actors tell a story that can touch us emotionally.

Singers do the same thing except with songs.

Billionaires become rich by selling products that usually improve the lives of their customers.

It's all connected.

Without you to watch the movie, an actor can't be popular.

Without you there to listen to a song, a singer will never gain recognition.

Without you buying a product, there will never be a billionaire.

The more you help others, the more you help yourself.

QUALITY #3 • THE CONFIDENCE QUALITY

How often in your life has someone told you that you need to be more confident?

But what does that mean?

Have you ever really stopped and thought about it?

Most of us assume that being confident is a state of being much like being "Ungettable."

But what if I were to tell you that being confident is a lot more simple than you could imagine.

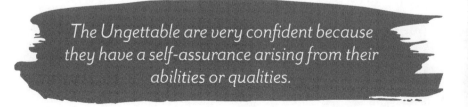

The Ungettable are very confident because they have a self-assurance arising from their abilities or qualities.

Essentially they feel that life can throw them a curveball, and no matter how difficult that curveball is, they can handle it.

But when we look at why the Ungettable are confident it isn't just because they have supreme confidence in their abilities, it goes deeper than that.

They feel confident they know the truth of things.

I firmly believe that some of the most intelligent people in history are philosophers.

SPECIFICALLY SOCRATES

In school, we are taught the scientific method.

Mainly you come up with a hypothesis, and then you experiment to either prove or disprove the hypothesis.

Well, what if I were to tell you that the scientific method stole from the Socratic method that Socrates came up with in 399 BC.

You see, Socrates was obsessed with finding the truth of things, and he came up with a framework to help him do that.

By asserting a thesis and doing everything you can to pick that thesis apart, you could slowly and methodically arrive at the truth of a thing.

In my experience, the Ungettable are consistently doing this with all aspects of their life except instead of trying to get to the truth of things they are always taking note of their qualities and looking for ways to improve.

They never look at themselves as a final product.

They are never satisfied.

In short, they are perfectionists.

Always seeking to improve what they deem to be the weakest aspect of themselves.

If they feel their lives lack something, they work to conquer that aspect.

We live in this society where results are expected immediately.

Never before have we been able to get results faster with the advent of Google and communication platforms like Facebook or Snapchat.

But this feeling of instant gratification has bred unrealistic expectations with regards to complex ideas like confidence.

There is no magic bullet for making you more confident.

It's not the type of thing where you can wake up one morning and think to yourself,

"You know what? I'm going to be more confident today."

Confidence is only gained through mastery.

That's the truth.

Identify the qualities in your life that you'd like to improve and improve them.

Of course, one huge issue remains.

THE TOMORROW PRINCIPLE

If you're anything like me, you can read a section like this, agree with everything, get really fired up and then say the fatal final words,

"Starting tomorrow, I'm going to do this."

Except when tomorrow comes, you come up with some other excuse.

Pretty soon weeks have gone by, and you stop caring at that point.

Now is the time to do something about being Ungettable.

Now is the time to make a difference in your life.

Don't put it off anymore.

Because you and I both know that if you do put it off, you won't ever do anything, and you'll be sitting alone one day wondering why your life is so unfair and why no one ever picks you.

I've been there.

I've cried my eyes out, wondering these exact things, and the problem

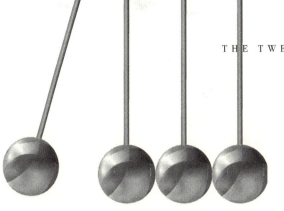

was that I was too lazy to slowly and methodically make myself into someone worth fighting for.

Here's the best piece of advice I can probably give you out of this entire book.

Action is always better than inaction.

Newton's first law of motion taught us that an object at rest stays at rest and an object in motion tends to remain in action with the same speed and the same direction unless acted upon by an unbalanced force.

The longer you sit still and don't do anything to conquer your fate, the more likely you are to sit still.

Move.

Get in motion.

Because once you start that motion, the more likely you are to stay in motion and create this snowball effect that will inevitably give you more confidence in all aspects of your life.

THE THREE LAYERS OF CONFIDENCE

Of course, I still haven't answered the most important question there is.

How does one make themselves more confident?

What can they do individually?

A woman can start with the mindset that she is going to be the best version of herself, but there's always something there that stops her from doing that.

This little internal voice of self doubt always holding her back from achieving real confidence.

Some women will tell themselves that they need to fake it, and eventually, they'll become confident, but it usually doesn't work out that way.

So, how can you become more confident in your life?

Well, a lot of what we've covered in this book is making inroads on teaching you how to do that, but I think it's essential to tackle the question head-on.

In my experience, there are three layers of confidence.

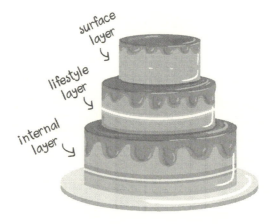

And they kind of work like a cake with each one stacked on top of each other.

But you'll find that one of the layers is far more critical than the others because you won't have a cake without it.

I'll explain that concept later.

First things first, let's take a look at the three layers.

THE FIRST LAYER: SURFACE LAYER

The first layer is all about perception. If you put some thought into it, how others perceive you can feed into your confidence.

This layer includes things like what you post on your social media accounts, how you look, how you walk, how you talk, basically anything external.

I think a significant argument can be made that this is the most superficial layer of confidence.

THE SECOND LAYER: LIFESTYLE LAYER

The first layer was all about how you look, act, and are therefore perceived.

This layer is all about what you do. What is your lifestyle like?

This can include skills, hobbies, work, family, and friends.

If you paid attention to the earlier chapters where I talked about the holy trinity, you might pick up on the fact that it falls into the lifestyle layer.

So, by mastering the three most prominent areas of your life, you can derive more confidence.

But again, I'd argue that while this is more important than the first layer, real confidence is not derived from being perceived a certain way or mastering the crucial areas and skills of your life.

It comes from a deeper place.

A deeper layer.

THE THIRD LAYER: INTERNAL LAYER

The internal layer is hard to describe, but easy to understand.

If you master this layer, you will feel emotionally invincible. It doesn't prevent you from having a painful experience, but it gives you the confidence to know that you'll be ok.

You can go through an awful breakup and know that everything will work out in the end.

How many of us can say that right now?

If someone or something took away the most important person in your life, whether that would be a friend, lover, or family member, would you be ok?

I wouldn't be emotionally ok, but I've been through enough to know that the experience would make me stronger.

A good life is not one immune to sadness but one in which suffering contributes to our development.

If there is wisdom to be taken from hard experiences, it lies in the understanding that the sorrow isn't just about you, that you have not been singled out, your suffering belongs to all of humanity.

To take that fully to heart is to become more compassionate and confident.

Here's the thing.

Mastering this internal layer of confidence doesn't happen in a day.

You aren't going to read this little section of the book and all of a sudden have this epiphany where you become extremely confident.

It's a process that can sometimes take years.

Of course, I realize I've been talking about the results of the internal layer of confidence without actually defining what it is.

Again, I want to reiterate that it is hard to describe, but the closest word I can think of to explain the internal layer is having high self-worth.

People who have an extremely confident demeanor understand that they are worth more.

But how can you develop this internal layer?

Well, there are two things you can do.

1. Shift the paradigm.
2. Work from the outside in.

My favorite concept in the world is the idea of the paradigm shift.

> *You are essentially training yourself to look at a set of circumstances in a new way.*

I'm so crazy about this concept that I have a shirt that says "shift the paradigm," except it's printed upside down.

It serves as a reminder that there's always a different perspective you can take on things.

Have you ever heard of the fable of the old Chinese farmer? It's a story told by philosopher Alan Watts.

The story is meant to help you understand that there's always a different perspective.

Now, I'm reciting from memory, so don't get too upset if I mess the story up.

Once upon a time, there was a farmer who lost a horse; it ran away.

That evening, all of his neighbors came around and said,

"My goodness, you lost your horse. How terrible."

The farmer said, "Maybe."

The next day the horse came back and brought seven wild horses with it.

The neighbors came again that night and said,

"How wonderful, your horse came back and brought seven more with it."

The farmer said, "Maybe."

The next day the farmers' son was attempting to tame one of the wild horses and was bucked off.

This resulted in a broken arm.

Once again, the neighbors came around and said,

"That's horrible; you should get rid of those horses since your son broke his arm."

The farmer said, "Maybe."

The next day the conscription officers came around to conscript his son into the army, but they couldn't do it because his son had a broken arm.

The neighbors came around again and said,

"How wonderful, he avoided the war."

The farmer gave his patented response, "Maybe."

Here's the point.

Entropy is the predominant force in all of our lives.

It's such a complex idea that it's impossible to determine whether anything that happens is good or bad.

There's always a different perspective that you can take when things look bad.

It's hard to realize that in the moment when hardship befalls you, but it's sometimes valuable to remember that you can always shift the paradigm.

The next concept I'd like to touch on is the idea of healing from the outside in.

This entire section has been about confidence, and it's three layers.

If you hadn't already noticed, I'm a big believer in this idea of synergy, of how working on one layer can benefit another layer without you realizing it.

I touched on this concept a little bit with the holy trinity, but you'll find it also applies here.

Sometimes the complexity of inner confidence can be complicated or intimidating.

So, instead of working on mastering it from the inside out, which most experts recommend, I do believe you can master it from the outside in.

By working on the external layers, you'll be able to get a few wins on the board and create momentum that you can swing to the internal layer.

QUALITY #4 • THE INTELLIGENCE QUALITY

Initially, I was going to name this "the witty quality," but after much debate, I determined that wit alone isn't what I wanted to capture, intelligence is.

Let me ask you a question.

What do you think matters most to a Ungettable person?

Physical beauty or intelligence?

I've already established that we are in a constant state of decay, looks fade.

Our minds do, too, for that matter.

So, what matters more to an Ungettable?

Intelligence!

Human beings are capable of amazing things, and it's not because of their attractive features.

Looks didn't order chaos.

Looks didn't bring man to the moon.

Intelligence did.

Here's the problem.

The media has made intelligence dull. One look at the magazines at your local grocery store will tell you that.

What are they featuring?

Celebrity diet tips?

Oh look, this celebrity broke up with that one.

We've been trained to care about vain things.

We've also been trained to hate reading, which upsets me.

What matters most is your mind.

And the only way to cultivate the mind is to read. It's what you are buying this book for.

We live in the golden age of information.

The internet is one big library that has answers for pretty much anything you might ever wonder.

Never before in human history has a creation like this existed.

And what are we all doing with it?

We are squandering it.

Many scientists believe that we have already reached the peak of human intelligence, and we are beginning to regress.

I'm not sure I necessarily agree with that, but what I do know is that we've been given access to something none of our ancestors had, and we should use it to its fullest potential.

Cormac McCarthy once said,

> "Books are all made from other books."

And if you think about it, it's entirely true.

In 1590, Thomas Kyd's The Spanish Tragedy was written.

In 1602, Antonio's Revenge was written.

Between 1599 and 1602, William Shakespeare writes Hamlet.

Each story is roughly about the same thing.

A man who wavers between madness after someone dear to him is murdered. Between his bouts of madness, he discovers who kills that someone dear and begins to plot his revenge.

In each play, there is a ghost begging for justice.

Each of these plays told the same exact stories with a few changes between them.

Shocked to hear that The Godfather Of English wasn't as original as you thought?

Technically speaking, Thomas Kyd's The Spanish Tragedy was written first, so shouldn't it get all the credit?

Well, not exactly.

Say what you want about Shakespeare, but the man could tell one hell of a story.

While the others told the same story first, Shakespeare did it better, and that's where I'd like to point you back to the Cormac McCarthy quote above.

"All books are made from other books."

That sums up the human race perfectly in my mind. All we know is the knowledge that we've accumulated from our ancestors.

Each generation takes the knowledge and improves upon it, so the future of our race can be secured.

There's something powerful about that concept.

So, what does any of this have to do with being Ungettable?

Aiming to learn everything you can about the things that genuinely interest you is attractive to everyone.

It gives you new things to teach when you go on dates.

It ensures that you always have something interesting to talk about.

Pretty soon, your friends, family, and romantic interests will listen when you speak because they know that when you do speak, you are always bringing something fascinating to the table.

The single biggest problem I see with my clients who struggle when they go on dates is that they can't carry a conversation.

Seeking to cultivate your mind takes care of that problem.

Of course, when you have access to the world's most extensive library on the internet, it can become a bit intimidating when it comes to choosing what to become more intelligent about.

I promise you it's not as complicated as I'm making it sound.

All you have to do is start by answering a straightforward question.

What are you passionate about?

For me, it's storytelling.

Besides writing books like this, which I kind of view as my outlet for explaining my philosophy on how to live, I want to write a fiction novel.

I want to write a story that captures the imagination and serves as my magnum opus.

Something that my daughter can pick up and read when she's older after I've passed away that can tell her all the things I can't express in person.

Every single night, after I'm done working, I study the art of writing a great story.

I've learned more about life and philosophy doing that than I did in college.

But it only works because I'm passionate about it.

It's also the reason I can come up with ridiculous facts like the William Shakespeare one above.

I would never have known that if I hadn't studied and learned about it for myself.

Cultivate your mind with the things that you are passionate about, and others will find you fascinating for it.

QUALITY #5 • THE LEAVE YOU WANTING MORE QUALITY

Here is where we move from the more philosophical applications into the practical ones.

Ten years ago, I was reading an article about how TV shows introduced cliffhangers and the reasoning behind them.

I found the whole topic fascinating.

It all dates back to 1927 when a woman named Bluma Zeigarnik learned that people remember uncompleted or interrupted tasks better than completed ones.

Her research gained some notoriety, and it was forever termed the Zeigarnik effect.

Mostly Hollywood took this concept and went to town on it with their TV shows.

If you think about it, traditional tv shows had one of the most difficult tasks imaginable.

They had to engage viewers and convince them to tune in again a week later when the next episode would air.

They learned that they had great success if they ended their shows on a cliffhanger or an unanswered question.

The cliffhanger had to be enticing enough for people to obsess over for a week to ensure they would tune back in to get their question answered.

Now, Netflix came in and shook things up with the advent of "binge-watching" tv shows, but if you pay attention, the Zeigarnik effect is still in play there.

Each Netflix show ends on some cliffhanger to ensure you watch "just one more."

Three hours later, you're staring at your phone, determining if it's ok to function with just four hours of sleep because you can't get enough of how excellent this experience is.

What does any of this have to do with being "Ungettable?"

Well, one clear pattern that I began to take note of when I took a look at individuals who were successful in dating is that they always seemed to leave people with this feeling of wanting more.

I've long held a theory that each conversation you have when you are trying to build attraction with someone will have a high point and a low point.

What tends to happen when you get excited about someone is you overstay your welcome, and the excitement of that conversation flattens out.

I'll give you a direct example from my own life.

When I met my wife for the first time, I couldn't get enough of her.

When we would talk on the phone, all I ever wanted to do was stay on the phone and learn everything I could about her.

Sometimes I would have to pinch myself because I couldn't believe I was falling for someone this much.

But an alarming trend started to develop.

As our conversations grew longer, they would grow staler. After all, there's only so much you can get to know about someone before you run out of things to talk about.

People who are "Ungettable" are excellent at not letting that happen.

They end conversations in the perfect place so that every experience ends on a cliffhanger.

It sounds simple.

Just ending a conversation at the right time shouldn't be that big of a deal.

But the goal is always to leave whoever you're interested in with this feeling that there is still more for them to uncover.

What begins to happen is that once you create a pattern of leaving your person wanting more, everything begins to open up for you.

They think about you more.

They contact you first.

They are more prone to emotional outbursts, where they tell you their feelings.

Sounds too easy, right?

Well, trust me when I say that it's not. The key is to establish a consistent pattern where you time the exact moment to exit conversations perfectly.

Let's talk about how you do that.

There are two elements that you need to keep track of.

1. When you are ending the conversation
2. How you end the conversation

I want to spend a minute or two to explain each of these elements so that you know exactly what you should be doing.

WHEN YOU END THE CONVERSATION

This element is all about timing and satisfaction.

One can't survive without the other.

You need whoever you are talking to, to be having a satisfying time before you end the conversation.

There's no cut and dry rule for determining this, so usually what I tell people is to feel it out with their gut.

If you're enjoying the conversation, there is a good chance that whoever you are talking to is as well.

Again, I'll use myself as a guinea pig for you.

When I'd be having those extremely long conversations with my wife on the phone, there would always be a moment where I'd internally think to myself,

"I don't want this conversation ever to end."

This internal thought would almost always happen between the 30 minute - 60-minute mark.

Usually, that's the optimal time to end the conversation.

It's not easy because if you're thinking,

"I don't want this to end."

You really won't want it to end.

HOW TO END THE CONVERSATION

If you thought that identifying when to end a conversation was difficult, then you're going to find this part even more challenging.

From what I have witnessed, there are two optimal ways in which one should end a conversation.

The first is also the most abrupt and can be sometimes viewed as rude.

If you are having the conversation over the phone, then simply hanging up the phone and pretending your battery went out is always effective.

Just ask my wife.

She used to pull this on me all of the time, and to this day, has never owned up to doing it on purpose, but I know it was all part of her plan.

I can't deny it's effectiveness, and I married her.

What's interesting about this approach is that even though it is totally rude, it is so sudden that often whoever you are having a conversation with is left with this feeling of wanting more, especially if you hung up and ended at the high point of the discussion.

The second way to end a conversation is to create an excuse for yourself to leave suddenly.

Dogs are effective here if you're on the phone or even in person.

"Oh shoot, I forgot to feed my dog and take him for a walk."

The key here is that the excuse needs to sound legitimate, and it needs to be urgent.

I don't think I need to dive much more into this concept.

Instead, let's end this section abruptly.

QUALITY #6 • **THE OUT OF YOUR LEAGUE QUALITY**

About seven years ago, I watched this fascinating documentary on attraction.

Mainly the documentary was nothing more than a bunch of experiments on how attraction is viewed and how we make decisions on picking life partners.

I learned some exciting things, but one experiment always stuck out to me.

A group of 30 individuals, 15 men, and 15 women were rounded up and given a number.

Each number was between one and ten.

The number was consistent with how others in the study viewed their "attractiveness level."

One being the lowest level of attractiveness and ten being the highest.

Here's where things begin to get fascinating.

Each participant in the study was given a special suit that covered their entire body, so only their face was visible. On each persons forehead was their attractiveness number.

So, you wouldn't be able to see your own "level of attraction," but you'd be able to see everyone else's.

Scientists were studying if similar levels of "attraction" would naturally pair up given a choice.

Each person in the study was given something like ten minutes to find a suitable partner to pair up.

Here's how it worked.

The men were able to make an outreach attempt, which would be signified by them outstretching their hand.

Only the women were able to accept the match by taking the hand.

There was also no talking allowed; scientists wanted to ensure this was only based on looks.

As the experiment played out, it was fascinating to watch women reject men who they felt were beneath them and how many "attempts" from men went to the most attractive individuals in the experiment.

After the ten minutes were up, each person was allowed to take the number off their forehead to see how they were rated and also see how close the numbers were to their partners.

It was almost uncanny how closely matched everyone was, the sevens paired with the sevens, the eights matched with the eights, and the fours matched with the fours.

There were a few that didn't match perfectly, but they weren't far off.

I think a six chose a seven and a four chose a five.

The result of the experiment was clear. Given a choice, if all things are equal, men and women of "equal attractiveness levels" will pair up.

And that's where I'd like to chime in.

In life, not all things are equal.

The experiment left out quite a few essential qualities to ensure that things were equal.

Participants weren't allowed to talk.

They weren't allowed to show off their bodies, remember only their faces were shown.

They also were handcuffed, so only men could make the "overtures."

I'm sure the results would have been entirely different had those things been allowed.

This chapter has been entitled "the out of your league" quality.

Have you wondered why that is?

Until this point, each Ungettable quality that we've explored has been kind of internal.

It's something that relates to you directly.

With this one, we are looking at the external. Specifically what men want when it comes to "looks" and how the Ungettable deal with that.

So, I'm going to tell you.

The Ungettable girl will inevitably make a man feel like she is out of his league.

This is why I brought up that study.

Even its imperfections.

Yes, looks play a role in making a man feel like the person he's dating is out of his league, but there are also other aspects to it as well.

I'll use myself as an example, and I'll be brutally honest with you.

I feel someone is out of my league if they are better looking than I am and more accomplished.

There are two elements to unpack here.

1. They have to be better looking than I am

2. They have to be more accomplished than I am

Let's dissect.

ELEMENT ONE: **THEY HAVE TO BE BETTER LOOKING THAN I AM**

Think of that experiment I cited at the beginning of this chapter.

Remember how I said that most of the time, the attractiveness levels matched up, but there were a few outliers.

In those particular circumstances, you had one person reaching and one person settling.

The reacher: the person is swinging above their weight class.

> *The settler: the person is picking below their weight class.*

The Ungettable always needs to be the settler in a man's eyes. He needs to feel like he got the deal of a lifetime.

Here's the most beautiful part of the whole concept.

The "settler" doesn't have to be so far above the reacher attractiveness wise.

Let's use the archaic number system that the experiment earlier did.

Let's say that you rate yourself as a seven out of ten.

If your guy is a six out of ten looks-wise, then he is the "reacher," and you are the settler.

Now, I'm sure some women are reading this who are panicking because, for whatever reason, they believe they aren't good enough.

There are two things I'd like to tell you.

Women are almost always better looking than men.

I'm sorry it's true.

And also, being "out of someone's league" isn't all about looks.

Remember, there were two factors you need to look at to achieve this quality.

The look was one, but being more accomplished was the other.

ELEMENT TWO: **THEY NEED TO BE MORE ACCOMPLISHED THAN I AM**

As I've grown older and more accomplished in my life, it becomes harder to impress me.

That's a natural part of growing older and becoming more cultured.

I find that I've become increasingly more drawn to people who have skills that I envy or have accomplished more than I have in my life.

Accomplishment can come in many forms.

Most people tend to jump to careers when I talk about this concept, but it's more than that.

Qualities, achievements, and stories tend to impress me more than anything now.

I admire my wife's ability to be selfless and care for others.

I idolize people who have achieved amazing things in the world and their careers.

I envy those who can tell stories.

This all matters to that "out of your league" feeling.

Why do you think I've spent so much time in this book talking about things outside of the "do this and make a man fall for you" realm?

The Ungettable realize that those types of shallow strategies work in the short term, sure, but they aren't what matter in the long term.

I think we've lost sight of that, but that's what I'm writing this book for, to help you see what matters when it comes to being the woman every man wants.

QUALITY #7 • THE ALWAYS BUSY QUALITY

A few chapters ago, I cited Newton's laws of motion.

Specifically, I zoned in on the first law.

> *"Every object in a state of uniform motion will remain in that state of motion unless an external force acts on it."*

Essentially get up, get moving, keep moving, and you'll be surprised at what you can accomplish.

But how does "always being busy" translate into being Ungettable.

Perception is everything.

And most women give off the perception that they are desperate if they are always available for a man.

In other words, they are too available.

I've spent the better part of ten years working with women trying to train them not to appear available to men.

To have more in their lives to keep them busy, so they aren't hanging on his every word or response.

It's difficult because many women are so desperate to find "the one" that they push too hard and appear too desperate.

When things inevitably fall apart, and they are left wondering why they are too wrapped up in the wrong things.

"I'm not good looking enough."

"He's going to find someone better than me."

"What's wrong with me?"

These internal negative beliefs create this false narrative that follows you around from relationship to relationship with each failure adding another "negative thought."

The more you live in that despair, the more desperate you become to fix your love life.

It's an endless self-perpetuating cycle that won't ever end until you have a paradigm shift.

Let me ask you a life question.

When it comes to your priorities, where does your love life fall?

Is it the most important thing to you?

Here's how you tell.

If you're engaged in an activity and something regarding your love life comes up, do you drop everything you are doing and focus on it?

If the answer is yes, then that means your love life is the most important thing to you.

Well, here's what I suggest.

Find something else, outside of your love life that you are so passionate about that can match your enthusiasm for falling in love and living happily ever after for some that can be work for others that can be physical fitness.

Whatever it is, all that matters is that you are passionate about it.

Earlier I talked about the concept of "the holy trinity," which is essentially what I deem to be three of the most important priorities that you should be focusing on throughout your everyday life.

If you can focus a little more on the aspects outside of your love life, you're going to find it helps your love life.

It sounds incredibly odd.

But the Ungettable have this down pat.

They understand that men aren't their only priority in the world.

And that bleeds through when they do converse with men.

Instead of having him think,

"Wow, this girl is super desperate."

He thinks,

"Wow, this girl is so busy."

Men want to be your primary focus. The best analogy I can think of to illustrate that point is that of a video game.

The worst video games are ones that are easy to beat.

They offer no challenge or resistance.

The same goes for women.

Those that tend to be available are easy to win over.

The ones that aren't are challenging, and that's intriguing.

Don't make it easy for men.

Find other priorities that you can focus on, so you aren't always at his beck and call.

QUALITY #8 • THE PLAYFUL QUALITY

One consistent quality that I found among women who are deemed Ungettable was the fact that they weren't afraid to show their playful side.

Being "playful" has many different connotations. For some, it means having a great sense of humor.

Others will claim that being playful means, you need to be "fun-loving."

I think that doesn't entirely take everything into account.

The Ungettable use "playfulness" as a way to flirt, and men love them for it.

Studies have long suggested that a woman who is considered playful by males have a higher propensity for displaying her youth and fertility, two things that matter to men.

The real problem with books like this is that when you are instructed to "be playful," everything seems forced.

What matters is that everything unfolds naturally.

So, how can one be naturally playful, so the best results are yielded with flirting?

The devil is in the details, after all.

So, here's what I'm going to do for you. I'm going to let you in on my super "not so secret" flirting formula.

Think of it as the ultimate framework you can fall back on to determine if you're playful or "flirty" in the right way.

DISSECTING THE FLIRTING FORMULA

Let's start by talking about what the actual formula is.

Many different experts have different ideas for what "creates" flirting, but after years of working with all kinds of clients, I think it boils down into two simple concepts.

Flirting = Attraction Built + Challenge

And I'm going to use a real example from my own life to illustrate this concept.

First things first, though, let's talk about the factors in my actual equation.

"Attraction built" equates to anything that catches someone's interest.

This can be something as simple as a flirty text or something more direct, like a sexy look across the way at a party. Anything that you do or say that makes someone more attracted to you can be plugged into the "attraction built" portion of the formula.

Pretty straightforward.

That's the part that most people can do easily.

The next part is where they fail nine times out of ten.

Presenting a "challenge" is what makes you Ungettable and different from the rest of the women in the world.

You see, most women only "build attraction" and expect that to work for them.

Sometimes it does.

But I'm not writing this book so that you are like most women. I want you to be extraordinary, and to do that; you need to make men jump through hoops to ensure that you are challenging to win.

How does one do that?

Allow me to illustrate.

The story I'm about to tell you may sound a bit odd, but I swear to you everything happened exactly how I'm about to explain it.

It also may be the single most exceptional example of "playfulness" I've ever seen.

When I was twenty-two years old, I was invited to go out to a bar from my friend.

He had signed up for that dating website, Plenty of Fish, and snagged a date.

The girl invited him to this line dancing bar about twenty miles away in

Galveston, Texas.

He was scared to make that drastic of a trip alone for some girl he had never met in person before.

He wanted backup, so he called the best person he knew, me.

In all actuality, I think I was his last choice, but my ego can't take that.

Anyways, we get there to the bar, and it's heavily cowboy themed.

Everyone is dressed up with cowboy hats, jeans, boots, and then you have us, two guys dressed up like a bunch of millennials sticking out like sore thumbs.

Eventually, he meets his date, and things don't go very well. The two of them don't click, probably because he was too afraid to come alone and brought me.

She leaves early, and while my friend is bummed, he is determined to salvage the night.

"Chris, why don't we stay and dance. Maybe we'll meet some chicks."

Now, there are two things you need to know about me.

I'm timid, and I don't dance.

This proposition sounded like the dumbest idea in the world, but it turned out to be pretty great for him, not for me.

You see, on the dance floor was our very own Ungettable girl. She seemed like a water dancer.

All the men gravitated towards her, and she played them all.

Dancing with this one, with that one, leaving each new man excited and each old one confused as to why she left.

My friend hadn't gone out to dance floor to try his luck because I refused to budge from the sidelines, but I'd be lying if I said we both hadn't noticed this Ungettable genie crumbling men left and right.

The more I watched her, the more I realized that she had a very distinct pattern.

She would dance with a guy, excite him and then move on to the next available partner.

She was beautiful, yes, but when I noticed her pattern, it told me she was also smart.

Women like this aren't necessarily rare; they are just unique, and every man in that bar was drawn to her for it.

Then she did something no one was expecting.

She broke from her pattern.

She started walking right towards me, what the hell was happening?

She looked at me.

I looked at her.

Could this be a connection?

As each step brought her closer, I began imaging what a relationship would be like with her.

I'd have to fight men off because she'd be hit on so much.

Worth the risk.

Here she is.

So close, I could touch her.

She reached her hand out.

Am I dreaming?

And that's when reality smacked me in the face as she grabbed my friend's hand and trotted him out to the dance floor.

She worked her magic on him.

I'd seen this before. It was the pattern.

Next, she would move on and find a different partner.

But it didn't happen.

They danced, and I just sat with my jaw on the floor at why he was chosen over me.

Was it my looks?

There's no way he is better looking than me.

What the hell happened?

While I was lost in my thoughts, my friend began making moves on her and secured her number.

What was I witnessing?

The grin on his face after they parted was enough to bridge a gaping hole in a dam.

"When should I text her?" He asked me.

"Well, wait until you leave the damn bar, at least."

He listened to that advice and texted her as I drove the two of us home.

His chosen message?

"Hey, it's Phillip from the bar."

That's where things got interesting.

If he was expecting to bond with this girl, his hopes were supremely dashed.

"Who?"

It was minutes before I stopped laughing.

But my friend's Ungettable ride wasn't over yet.

After a few minutes, she promptly added to the texting thread,

"Oh right, you're that super cute guy I danced with last."

Things were back on track for my friend, and I was thoroughly impressed; this girl had game.

That's where I'd like to end my story and start applying the flirting formula.

For those reading, if you already have forgotten what the formula is it's,

Flirting = Attraction Built + Challenge

So, where was attraction built?

Technically speaking, the Ungettable girl built the attraction the second she started captivating us with her "water dancing."

At least, that's what I'm going to call it because that's what it felt like.

For my friend attraction was built the second, she took his hand to dance with him.

So many thoughts must have been going through his head during that moment.

Is this real?

She picked me out of all these guys.

Did someone dare her to do this?

I can't believe this is happening to me.

But technically speaking she isn't ungettable here. I think an argument can be made she is the opposite of ungettable.

She is "gettable."

Notice how my friends' confidence in winning her over all the guys had grown to the point that he was the only one to secure her phone number.

He had grown so confident that he wanted to text her right away to solidify his position further.

She's still "gettable."

And that's when she throws him a roadblock.

Or if we are going to use my terminology.

That's where she introduces the challenge.

All my friend knows before he texts this girl is the following,

- She's the hottest chick at the bar
- She's an awesome dancer
- She chose him over all the other guys
- She gave him her number

Things are looking good.

So, my supremely confident friend texts her with the most generic text you could imagine.

"Hey, it's Phillip from the bar."

In his mind, she is what you would call a one night stand.

The kind of girl that he'd sleep with and lose interest in.

And it's all shaping up nicely for him until that challenge is introduced in the form of a straightforward word.

"Who?"

Every preconceived notion my friend had about her comes tumbling down.

He thought he was special.

The one guy she picked out of all the other guys in the bar.

That one-word message disproved that.

It just means he was part of the pattern. One of the guys she left behind in the wake of her path.

It's at this point that most men give up or grow angry.

Why?

Because they've lost control.

But that's when the girl does something incredibly intelligent.

She texts him again, with a compliment.

"Oh right, you're that cute guy I danced with last."

Hope has returned.

But he needs to be careful.

This girl won't be easy to get.

It was the single most magnificent display of playfulness and flirting I've ever seen.

You see, most women make the mistake of believing ungettable is the same thing as impossible.

They're not.

The ungettable girl can be "won" just not quickly.

The trick lies in how you approach flirting and communication.

Most people are straightforward.

They play checkers.

The ungettable play chess.

You see, I think the girl always intended to give my friend a compliment.

I think she picked him out because he caught her eye, and she did want to pursue things with him.

But she knew she was maybe a little too straightforward in her approach, so she had to do something to catch him off guard.

She knew she couldn't seem too available.

So, she pretended not to know him.

She played with his emotions.

She must have known he'd be riding high after their dance. She must have known he'd be confident.

She also knew that if she could show him how she had control over his emotions, it would demonstrate a value no other average woman could match.

It's absolutely brilliant.

Think of his emotional state throughout that three text exchange.

He starts confidently when he sends his introductory text.

But that quickly changes into being upset when he realizes that she didn't even remember him.

A few minutes later, that emotional state changes again into happiness but not quite as confident.

All because she knew how to use the flirting formula to be playful.

QUALITY #9 • THE SEXY QUALITY

I want to handle this quality with care because I think there is a fundamental misunderstanding that women have about being sexy.

Sex is a physical act.

Everything about it is physical.

But that has nothing to do with what I want to talk about in this chapter.

> *Too often, women believe that the missing piece to the puzzle to capture the man of their dreams has to do with sex.*

"I'm not good looking enough."

"He won't be interested in me if I don't sleep with him."

"I'm going to be stuck in the friend zone if we don't take the next step."

What the ungettable understand perhaps better than anyone is that creating sexual tension with the man you are interested in is the key from turning a friendship into a relationship.

The problem is most women I meet don't know how to create sexual tension.

They can be good at it.

They're just scared at how they'll be perceived.

So, let's start with the basics.

When do you know that it's ok to take a very early friendship into more "flirty" tension-filled waters?

Most women worry that a man will only look for sex if they do that too early, but I disagree entirely.

I think the sooner you can create the tension, the better.

Why?

Because it can kind of serve as a filtering system to determine just how interested the guy is in you.

What's interesting is there is kind of a mirror effect going on here.

Most women are terrified of being shut down.

But most men are too.

So, what happens most of the time is you have two parties in this endless standoff where nothing is getting done, and things fizzle out.

So, here's the million-dollar question.

How does one create sexual tension?

Well, it's simple.

You are going to use words that imply sex.

This is a technique that you can use at any stage of the attraction process.

It can work in text messages.

It can work on the phone.

It can even work in person.

Communication is the key to attraction, whether you realized it or not.

By using words that have some connection to sex, you'll be surprised at how powerful it is.

I'll give you a few examples.

Let's say you are texting a guy, and you want to create some sexual tension.

What can you say without giving away too much?

Well, let's look at some of the words that you can use that implies sex.

- Hot
- Cute
- Blushing
- Sexual
- Handsome
- Shower

All these words have some connection to sex and, if appropriately used in text messages, can create a killer combination.

Here's one that worked for one of my clients.

You say, "I had a dream about you last night."

This is what I refer to as a great hook.

It's an unanswered question that a guy has to find the answer to so he can't help but respond.

He says: "What happened?"

To which you reply, "I'm not telling, but I'll say this. It made me blush."

There's a reason I structured the book to have a playful quality before the sexy quality.

There's a fascinating synergy between the two.

Notice in the text example we used the flirting formula.

We said something to create interest or desire with the dream and created a challenge by not telling the guy what it was. Instead, we worked some sexual tension in.

It all connects.

Of course, using words that imply sex isn't the only way to create sexual tension.

Let's switch gears and talk about something physical that you can do.

For this, I'd like to tell you a story.

I was a bit of a late bloomer.

I didn't have my first date until I was 18 years old, and the entire event was terrifying for me.

Her house was a good 10 - 15 miles away from mine, and I got lost on the way there.

I had just started driving.

Eventually, when I did find her house, I met her father, who scared me like no other man.

When our date began, I remember physically shaking from stress and worry.

She must have sensed it, and she did something that, to this day, made an incredible impression on me.

She started telling a story.

I don't know if she intended to get my mind off of the stress or not, but she did this fantastic thing.

As she would tell the story, she would illustrate important parts by touching my shoulder or leg.

That little physical touch calmed me down completely and created the beginnings of sexual tension.

She was not aware of the touches; I'm sure of that. It was just embedded in her personality.

So, how can you use this to your advantage and create sexual tension?

Just do exactly what my ex did.

When you tell fantastic stories illustrate the crucial points by touching your man's shoulders or legs.

By now, you should be noticing a trend.

Less is more when it comes to sexual tension.

And this is something I've struggled to explain to women for years.

They are too direct in how they create tension.

Earlier I told you that I'm passionate about storytelling, and there's a story that I think fits our needs though it might sound a little strange at first.

Have you ever seen Steven Spielberg's Jaws?

If not, do yourself a favor and watch it.

One thing you'll notice about the movie is that Spielberg makes a very conscious decision to build up the tension and terror of the shark but never really shows the shark in its full glory until the very end.

He understood that the audience was going to be a lot more engaged if they felt a constant tension from scene to scene, and giving away the shark would break that tension.

That's kind of how sex needs to be treated with men.

It needs to be a constant presence in the background that men are thinking about but can't ever quite grasp.

You make it a constant presence by utilizing sexual tension.

Determining when to sleep with a guy is entirely up to you. I have an opinion, which is that you probably shouldn't show the shark until you have a man in a committed relationship, but I'm not going to push that view on you.

Your fate is your own.

You're ungettable after all.

QUALITY #10 • THE NURTURE QUALITY

This may initially seem like an odd quality to highlight in an ungettable girl, but it matters.

You'll always hear me talking about paradigm shifts, and I think it's a fundamental concept for you to grasp.

All I'm ever trying to get you to do is to have one moment where the lightbulb goes off, and things click.

Often that can't happen without you looking at things from a different perspective.

What I'm about to say may initially seem odd but will make total sense if you look at it from a different perspective.

There's a specific part of every man that genuinely wants a new mother. Let that sink in for a moment.

> *What he wants is someone to mother him and love him unconditionally.*

Psychologists will often label this as "mother issues," but I'm not entirely sure that is true.

If a man had a fantastic upbringing and childhood, he'd be seeking the nurturing quality in his partners because that has been the status quo since the beginning.

If a man did not have that fantastic upbringing, he'd still be seeking someone nurturing to fill a void that has never been filled before.

This is where attachment styles enter the equation, and I'm sure experts in those areas can poke holes in my "nurture/mother" theory, but from what I've observed, it exists.

I think the disconnect or disagreement occurs because women take it to the extreme too often.

How often have you been in a relationship only to be broken up with even though you were "nurturing."

Well, maybe the problem is that you were too nurturing.

He wants someone who has the qualities of his mother, not someone who is his mother.

It's an essential and often overlooked distinction.

So, how does one create the ideal balance when it comes to "nurturing qualities?"

I want you to take a look at each of the "ungettable qualities" I've talked about so far throughout this book.

No one is expecting you to master all of these qualities.

I think a strong argument can be made that it's impossible to become perfect in all of them.

In most cases, you'll find that women who attempt to master the twelve ungettable qualities can only truly master three or four.

That's not to say that they aren't satisfactory in the other qualities, they are.

It's just to truly master something you have to be excellent at it.

Nurturing is kind of like that.

You need to show that you are capable of nurturing, but you also need to ensure that you aren't nurturing all of the time.

Marriage has taught me that more than anything.

My wife is incredibly nurturing. Sometimes I'll look at her and think she was made to nurture others.

She is so selfless, and I always admire that.

Mostly because I feel sometimes I am too selfish.

But even though I witness her nurturing others, she doesn't always nurture me.

Sure, if I'm sick or under the weather, she'll nurture the hell out of me.

But when there's a work problem, I can't solve or some other element of life that I can't think of at this moment she'll leave me alone to answer it for myself.

She understands what every good parent should understand.

The greatest gift a parent can give a child is making them strong as opposed to protecting them from every little thing they may encounter.

I'm a voracious reader of fiction, so forgive the analogy I'm about to make.

Have you ever read Cormac McCarthy's "The Road?"

Maybe you've seen the movie.

It's without a doubt one of the darkest books I've ever read, but one of the most prominent themes of the book is that of parenthood.

Throughout the entire book, the man is slowly preparing his child to face the difficult world without him, a prospect that frightens any parent.

After all, anyone who is a parent or has held an infant in their arms knows first hand how fragile these little human beings are.

It's completely natural to want to protect a child with everything you possibly have.

But sometimes if you are too overprotective, the child won't be prepared for the hardships that life will throw it's way when it gets older.

It's something I struggle with all the time with my daughter.

I literally held her and protected her as an infant. I was there when she had to get surgery as an infant.

I stayed up all night with her for two days in a row during and after that surgery.

I'm the protector.

That's what I'm good for.

But a protector isn't an "over protector."

I think that this is a perfect sentiment that needs to be applied to relationships and nurturing.

What is nurturing if not protecting and caring for another human being?

That doesn't mean you do it all the time.

You do it in flashes and spurts.

You show men that you are capable of being nurturing, but you aren't here to nurture all day every day like most mothers.

QUALITIES 11 AND 12 • THE MYSTERY AND STABILITY QUALITIES

I put these two qualities together for a particular reason. There has always been an exciting synergy between stability and mystery.

But more on that in a second.

First things first, what do I mean when I talk about stability and mystery?

> With stability, I'm referring to being a stable force that can be relied upon in a relationship.
>
> With mystery, I'm talking about the adventurous and spontaneous force of a relationship.

For the last ten years, I've worked with hundreds of individuals who have been through breakups.

What always shocks me is how applicable this ungettable quality is to most of their situations.

What I've found is that generally, when you look at breakups, people veer more towards one end of the spectrum and completely disregard the other.

The most common example I can think of is a relationship that started wholly adventurous and spontaneous but turns dull and boring.

In essence, you had a relationship that began on a foundation of mystery and turned into one wrought with stability.

That wasn't what was promised when the relationship started.

Of course, there are two sides to this coin.

You always have those couples that are incredibly stable, and then some event occurs, and one member wants to do more exciting things.

MYSTERY   **STABILITY**

This causes problems if both parties aren't on the same page.

So, the million-dollar question is, what is more important to have in a relationship?

Mystery or stability?

It's a trick.

You need both.

Too much of one thing kills the relationship, just like not enough of one can kill it.

This is what women who are ungettable understand without really consciously realizing it.

They know that true mastery lies in balancing these two opposing forces.

You've heard of the Yin and Yang Chinese philosophy, where two seemingly opposite or contrary forces may be interconnected and complementary.

Essentially mastering only one side of the stability and mystery curve won't be as powerful as focusing on both.

Here's the exciting thing.

In your heart, you know that you feel more comfortable on one side of the scale than the other.

Take me; I'm more comfortable on the stability side. It's not that I can't do adrenaline-filled things or be spontaneous or create mystery; it's that I don't feel as comfortable doing it as I do just being stable.

But being only stable isn't great for my relationships. It's predictable and boring.

You need to inject some excitement every once in a while.

Think of it like this.

When you watch a movie, do you enjoy it because you are watching something safe?

Absolutely not; the most celebrated movies are filled with conflict, plot twists, intrigue, and mystery.

But too much of those qualities eventually become too much or too ridiculous.

You see, a basic Hollywood rule of thumb is that every scene most contain a "turn" virtually a point in the scene where there is value change in emotion.

A character enters the scene in a particular emotional state, and by the end of the scene, that emotional state needs to have changed.

Next time you watch a traditional movie, I want you to pay attention and see if you can identify the turn.

Usually, it'll be a simple emotional switch between positive to negative or negative to positive.

However, what's interesting is that if you make these emotional value changes too frequently or too visible, the movie becomes unwatchable or becomes a straight-up comedy.

Serious filmmakers will take care to ensure that the significant emotional value changes happen in the most critical moments of the story, and the small ones lead up to those crucial moments.

This is how you need to view your relationships with people.

Except instead of emotional value changes, you're going to be using stability and mystery.

It's ridiculous if you do something stable like sitting on the couch and watching movies with your partner all day only to go out and skydive the next.

Sure, maybe that sounds exciting at first, but it's unrealistic to keep this level of intensity up.

Instead, I've found that the ungettable tend to be mostly stable with mystery injected in the more critical moments of the relationship.

Usually, those moments happen during things like important events or dates.

You do something extremely exciting with the intent of making your partner put the emotions they are feeling onto you.

This is a psychological concept called "misattribution of emotions."

Here's how it works.

When you do something exciting with someone, and they feel all kinds of incredible emotions, they are likely to attribute the feelings they are feeling in the moment to the person they are on the date with.

Don't be ok with just being stable or mysterious.

Be both.

Twelve

Regret and The Ideal Self

I don't want to sound too morbid, but we are all going to die. It's the natural way of things.

I believe it was Steve Jobs who once said,

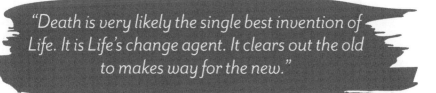

"Death is very likely the single best invention of Life. It is Life's change agent. It clears out the old to makes way for the new."

That quote is brilliant.

I'm weird, so for some strange reason, one of the things that fascinate me the most is what people say or think when they are on their deathbeds.

What are their regrets?

What in their last moments would they have changed?

Maybe I find it fascinating because it's a situation that I can learn from.

I don't know what the meaning of life is. Though the longer I live, the more I have this sneaking suspicion that the meaning is to live life to it's fullest.

I think there's a lot of insight we can get from others who are about to pass away.

They've lived their lives, and yet they have all these regrets.

A few years ago, a study was released by Cornell about the biggest regrets people have.

What they found fascinated me.

72% of participants of the study cited that they regretted not becoming their "ideal self."

WHAT IS THE IDEAL SELF?

In a perfect world, what would your life look like?

What job would you have?

Who would you be dating or married to?

These are all questions relating to the ideal self.

In other words, assuming everything worked out perfectly for you, what would you be like?

It seems most people regret things relating to this concept.

In psychology, the real self and the ideal self are terms used to describe how human beings view themselves.

The real self is who we are.

Things like how we think, feel, look, and act are all included to create this identity.

What's interesting is that since we have no way of viewing ourselves from an external perspective, the real self is a self-identity that we can only assign to ourselves.

In other words, it's our self-image.

The ideal self, on the other hand, is how we want to be.

An idealized image that we have developed over time based on what we have learned and experienced.

The goal should always be to make the real self and the ideal self align.

Doing this creates balance and a sense of mental well being that can't be matched.

If the ideal self and the real self aren't aligned, that's when you get things like regret and mental distress.

And now, we come full circle to the deathbed concept I was talking about at the beginning of this chapter.

Most people regret things relating to their ideal self.

The opportunities missed.

This only really happens when their self-image is not aligned with their idealized version.

The perspective I want you to have in life after you read this book is that you are going to live it without regrets.

Again, I hate to keep quoting Steve Jobs, but I think that there is a lot of truth to what he has to say.

> "Remembering that I'll be dead soon is the most important tool I've ever encountered to help me make the big choices in life. Because almost everything — all external expectations, pride, all fear of embarrassment or failure - these things fall away in the face of death."

I wonder what you would do differently in your life if someone told you that you only had a few months left to live?

It's a scary thought to even put out there in the universe, but the sword of Damocles has been hanging over all of our heads from the moment we were all born.

Death is what gives life meaning.

A compelling argument can be made that regret is simply a symptom of knowing our time is limited.

I don't claim to have all the answers, but I tend to think that the priorities in many of our lives would be different if we knew our exact expiration date.

So, here's my challenge to you if you want to be ungettable if you want to be attractive to others.

Sit and think about your priorities. Think about how you're spending your time.

Will you regret it in the end?

If the answer to that question is yes.

It's time to change the paradigm.

Thirteen

The 80/20 Rule

If you distill this book down to its purest form, the foundation upon which everything is built are the twelve ungettable qualities.

Without them, this is just one of those standard "hey improve your life" books.

Here's the thing.

I've already gone on record saying that I think it's close to impossible for you to master all the qualities.

Remember, to truly master something, it'll take 10,000 hours, and if you want to master each of the twelve qualities truly, that will take you approximately 120,000 hours, which is the equivalent of 13.7 years.

I don't know about you, but I certainly don't have thirteen years' worth of free time outside of spending time with my family, career, and essential going ons.

It's just not realistic to master each of the qualities.

I've also gone on record saying that you should choose qualities that are important to you.

But I was a little coy about the process you should use to do those things.

Have you ever heard of the 80/20 rule?

"In the most basic form, it shows us that 80% of our results come from 20% of our assets."

Human beings tend to fall for what I like to call "the shiny object" syndrome.

They see something cool or get an alluring idea and immediately set out to buy that cool thing or make that cool idea into a reality.

Halfway through doing a good job on that cool idea, they get another one and stop everything they are doing to pursue that new idea.

Over time they rinse and repeat this process, and pretty soon, they've spread themselves so thin that they haven't achieved anything.

The ungettable qualities are a little like that.

You'll read about all these fantastic things you can do to attract men, and you'll spread yourself too thin so that you haven't ever really mastered any quality.

Think of the ungettable qualities as weapons.

If you master a weapon, it can be wielded with excellent results.

However, if you don't master it, you can be taken down by a mere pebble assuming a master threw it.

Quality often trumps quantity, and that's the problem you are facing here.

But which weapons should you use?

Well, that's where the 80/20 rule comes into play.

Many times the 80/20 rule will be used by business owners who spread themselves too thin, but I find it applies to almost all areas of life.

But for simplicity's sake, let's use a business example to illustrate the 80/20 rule.

I am the owner of four different businesses.

I have a business teaching women how to handle breakups called Ex Boyfriend Recovery.

I also have a business teaching men how to handle breakups called Ex Girlfriend Recovery.

Then there is my save your marriage business called "Marriage Recovery."

Finally, I have a business helping women obtain the relationship they've always wanted with the man of their dreams.

This business is called "Ungettable."

Sound familiar?

Now, the cool thing about "Ungettable" is that it can be applied no matter the circumstance you find yourself in.

If you want to get your ex back, ungettable works.

If you want to get over your ex, ungettable works.

If you want to save your marriage, guess what?

Ungettable works.

When you have four businesses, you tend to get distracted very easily.

Often I find that I'm pulled in all sorts of different directions with that shiny object syndrome.

A few years ago, I falsely believed that it was possible to run these businesses effectively simultaneously.

After years of trying to do this, I concluded that I couldn't do a good job on any of them.

Instead, the job I was doing was mediocre on all of them.

This is when I sat back and decided that I was going to apply the 80/20 rule.

I started looking at the business in monetary terms.

Where was most of the money coming from?

Where was I having the most success?

To that point, each of the businesses was worth roughly 25% of my time.

So, by that measure, it probably meant that there would be one business that was generating most of the money, right?

It turns out, that was it exactly.

My business helping women through breakups was essentially holding most of my business upon its merit alone.

Therefore, it makes the most sense for me to spend most of my time and energy working to "master" that business.

Once that business is mastered, I could then move on to the next one and master that.

The ungettable qualities will probably work the same way.

In all, there are twelve qualities.

If you spread your time out equally among all twelve, that would mean that each one is worth about 8.3% of your time.

I don't know about you, but that doesn't seem like a lot of time to master any of the qualities.

Let's apply the 80/20 rule.

We know that 20% of the qualities are probably going to create 80% of the results.

The question you have to answer at this time is which ungettable qualities in your life have you found been most successful with men.

Every person reading this book will likely have a set of different qualities that they've seen success with.

Don't be alarmed. That's completely normal.

Generally speaking, if we stick to the 80/20 rule, that means you are going to want to focus on two or three of the following qualities.

1. The Daydream Quality
2. The Popularity Quality
3. The Stability Quality
4. The Mystery Quality
5. The Nurture Quality
6. The Sexy Quality
7. The Playful Quality
8. The Always Busy Quality
9. The Out of Your League Quality
10. The Leave You Wanting More Quality
11. The Confidence Quality
12. The Intelligence Quality

It's important that out of the two or three you choose that you don't get hung up on semantics and choose something that sounds romantic.

We are looking for qualities that will net you immediate results.

No offense to the nurturing quality, but that's probably something that you'll get more mileage out of when you enter into a relationship with someone.

Make these considerations for whatever your overall goal is.

Part Five

To Get The Guy You Need To Be Willing To Lose The Guy

"Life is really simple, but men insist on making it complicated"

-Confucius

Fourteen

Stop Putting Men On Pedestals

I titled this book Ungettable - Becoming The Woman Every Man Wants because it's ideal for marketing purposes.

Most of the women I work with want to know the secret to mastering men.

In their minds, they've built men up to be the key to life, but that's the wrong way to look at it, in my opinion.

It gives men too much credit and power.

And I think there's already too much of that to go around in the world.

You must stop putting men on pedestals.

You see, by putting men on this pedestal in your mind. By raising them to a godlike status, it creates this situation where you are easily intimidated by them.

You hang on their every word and syllable.

If they respond to you quickly in a text message, you're jumping with joy.

If they don't, you're depressed.

Now, I've been thinking for a long time about how to use an analogy to drive this point home, and after days of considering, I think I accidentally stumbled into the perfect one.

Professional tennis is one of those rare sports where every once in a while, an outlier will come in and upset the balance of what you think is accurate only to point out that it isn't true at all.

What do I mean by that?

The three greatest men's tennis players of all time are all playing on the tour right now.

In tennis, you aren't usually measured by how many tournaments you have won.

I mean, you are, but what matters more than anything are the grand slam tournaments.

There are four every year.

- The Australian Open.
- The French Open.
- Wimbledon.
- The US Open.

Three men have dominated these tournaments in my lifetime, and now that all three of them are on the backend of their careers, we are seeing something fascinating happening.

They are playing players that are drastically younger than they are, more on that in a second.

So, who are these three gods of tennis?

Roger Federer.

Rafael Nadal.

Novak Djokovic.

These three men have single handily fought off challengers from three different eras.

The old era.

Their era.

And the new era.

The most impressive part of the whole thing is the fact that they are now beating players significantly younger than them. Often you'll hear before one of their matches that their opponent grew up watching them.

In other words, they've idolized them.

As young children, they probably muttered things like,

"I want to be like Rafa when I grow up."

As young adults, they probably think,

"I want what Roger has."

I think a significant argument can be made that this exact mindset causes the new generation to lose.

Why?

They are putting the big three on a pedestal and idolizing them.

Sure, the big three have successfully beaten men from each generation.

But what is rare is a new generation faltering.

That usually doesn't happen in tennis.

If you look historically, you'll usually notice that the great champions can beat the old era (because they're the new kids on the block) and can beat their own generation.

But they usually aren't able to beat the new generation because at that point they've become older and it's someone else's turn.

That's what makes the greatness of Novak, Rafa, and Roger so fascinating.

We are watching them take advantage of their idolization.

It's a lesson I hope you take.

The more you idolize a man, the more power you give him, and we know that men aren't always great when they have power.

Fifteen

Leverage

Life is about leverage, whether you realize it or not.

Generally, whoever has the leverage will get their way while the person without leverage will not.

But does this apply to attraction and dating?

Well, yes, but not in the way you are probably thinking.

This whole book has been about turning you into the very best version of yourself.

It's touched on philosophy, game theory, and motivation.

The end goal is obviously to become so attractive that you naturally draw people to you.

In essence, it's all about gaining you leverage over men by inspiring you to be the ultimate version of yourself.

But what are you supposed to do when you gain leverage?

Well, that's ultimately up to you, but I can tell you what most women want to do.

They want to make a man commit to them.

But even despite having the leverage, they don't know how to do that.

I'll be honest, when I first started Ex Boyfriend Recovery and Marriage Recovery I didn't know either.

But over the years, you learn by watching what works and what doesn't work.

And that's what I'm going to show you right now.

I'm going to teach you how to use your leverage correctly by showing you five concepts that explain how men make commitment decisions.

So, if you master these five things, you're in good shape.

But I'd like to go further down the rabbit hole by dividing these five concepts into two categories.

1. The concepts that make a man want to commit to you

2. The concepts that make a man take action and commit to you

Let's tackle the concepts that make a man want to commit to you first.

CATEGORY 1 • THE CONCEPTS THAT MAKE A MAN WANT TO COMMIT TO YOU

Human beings tend to commit to one another on cost and benefit scenarios.

Mainly they're always looking to maximize the benefits and minimize the costs.

Don't be fooling yourself.

At each point during the dating phase, they're always looking to see if there's a better deal out there.

Now, the million-dollar question is on what scale are they grading?

What are the factors they are looking at or paying attention to?

There's three.

1. Satisfaction - how satisfied they are in the relationship

2. Alternatives - can anyone meet their needs better than you

3. Investment - how much time, money, emotional energy have they invested

What's interesting is that not all of these factors are created equally.

When scientists have done studies, they've found that even if someone scored poorly in the "satisfaction" and "alternatives" portion of the big picture, a person could still stay in a relationship if they feel that they've invested too much time and energy into it.

So, how does this help you gain leverage?

Well, do you remember why I divided these concepts up into two categories?

This is the category that only makes someone want to commit to you.

Want is different than need.

In every relationship you have from this point on in your life, I want you to do constant checks where you score yourself based on satisfaction, alternatives, and investment.

In a perfect world, you want to leave a man satisfied, feeling there's no one out there better than you and that they've invested so much time into you that they can't go anywhere else.

Of course, wanting to commit to you is different than needing to commit to you.

CATEGORY #2 • THE CONCEPTS THAT MAKE A MAN NEED TO COMMIT TO YOU

There are only two concepts you need to learn about here.

And they are basic sales strategies.

1. Scarcity
2. Urgency

What's more interesting about these concepts is that they are interrelated.

By successfully accomplishing one, you achieve the other.

But how?

Let's tackle "scarcity" first.

What is scarcity, and how can you show it?

Scarcity is nothing more than showing to someone that you are one of a kind.

That there is no one else out there in the world like you.

Essentially, zigging when every other woman zags.

It's what I've been teaching you to do throughout this entire book.

But what about urgency?

Urgency is nothing more than giving someone an urgent reason to want to commit to you.

How does that work?

Simple, this is where you apply the leverage I've been talking about in this chapter through fear of loss.

If a man doesn't act now, he'll lose you forever.

Most women take this to mean that an ultimatum needs to be given for the leverage to be applied.

In my experience, ultimatums don't work.

So, I'll give you the best piece of advice on how to create an extreme sense of urgency to make a man want to commit to you.

Show, don't tell.

Have the man you want see other men fawn over you.

Have him see you go on dates with them.

Have him worry that one of these other men will capture your heart and take you away forever.

Make him think that if he doesn't act, he won't get the woman he wants, you. The beautiful part about all of this is that if you strive to be ungettable other men, including the one you want, will naturally be drawn to you.

It all works together.

Sixteen

From Men; The Perfect Woman

Thus far, we've talked about some big concepts, and I'm sure most of you reading are all in on the idea of becoming ungettable.

But there may be a few who need an extra nudge.

You might be skeptical that all of this even works. So, I thought it would be interesting to ask men a singular question,

"Describe your perfect woman."

And see how inline their ideal woman is with the twelve ungettable qualities.

I know I've made a big deal about the fact that some men don't know what they want until you show it to them, but ultimately as you'll learn is that what they struggle with is putting what they want into words.

It's all there. You just have to look carefully.

In all, I'm going to cite from six men and point out which ungettable qualities they are attracted to from their mouths.

MAN #1 • KEVIN

"My dream girl consists of a pretty girl of course, who loves to laugh a lot. Has a sense of humor and doesn't take life so serious. She would be athletic

(take care of herself). Being spontaneous is a plus too."

Like I said, most men know what they want. They just can't explain it.

Kevin's thoughts here are all over the place.

He wants his girl to be pretty and laugh a lot.

He also wants her to have a sense of humor, which means he values this quality since he mentioned laughing and humor so close together.

The athletic portion I think can fit with his ideal girl being pretty.

He also cited being spontaneous as a big plus, which fits into the "mystery" part of ungettable.

In all, when you look at Kevin's dream woman, there are three qualities he favors.

1. She needs to be good looking
2. She has to have a sense of humor
3. She needs to be spontaneous.

Immediately three ungettable qualities are highlighted here.

The good looking quality fits right in with the "out of your league quality."

The sense of humor might fall nicely under the playful ungettable quality.

And of course, spontaneous behavior is connected to the mystery quality.

So, we are three for three in those ungettable qualities so far.

Let's see if this trend holds.

MAN #2 • MICHAEL

"When I see my dream girl I envision sunshine. Opening my eyes in the morning and seeing a radiant smile. I see a supportive best friend and

someone I can rely on and be present for as well. I see someone who is full of life and passion. Someone who doesn't get discouraged during trying times and finds the good in everything. I see a woman that I can lock eyes with across the room and we can share the same thought without sharing a word. A woman of great virtues to pass onto our children. And a woman that I can sit next to when we're older and laugh at all the great moments we shared throughout our years."

What I found fascinating about Michael's dream girl is how lovely she sounds.

She seems like sunshine.

Moments where the two lock eyes are envisioned.

Future visions crop up often with their imaginary children.

Michaels dream woman is a daydream. If you read his entire answer, he literally told you his perfect fantasy.

This fits nicely with ungettable quality #1, the daydream quality.

Let's move on.

MAN #3 • JOHN

"My dream girl is a girl that accepts me for who I am, we don't necessarily have to have everything in common, I actually prefer for us to have our own hobbies but be supportive of one another. Most importantly a strong personality that our relationship would be complimenting each other's lifestyles more than dependent."

I like John.

Not once in his description did he mention looks.

He's a man who prioritizes personality and independence more than anything.

If you look closely, you will notice that there are two

ungettable qualities that he seems to like.

The always busy quality jumps to mind immediately. This is apparent when he mentions that his dream girl needs to have her own hobbies and be independent.

What I also sense through reading his write up is that he values stability.

He wants someone he can rely on and be there for him.

MAN #4 • KYLE

"A smart with a college education, very nice and loving. Puts my needs before hers and will do anything to make me happy. Has a good moral background and has family values. Wants to have kids and a family. A girl who will always appreciate what I do for her no matter how little or big. About 5'2 115 pounds. Goes to the gym and stays fit. Has a toned body. Nice breasts like a c cup. Perfect white teeth and amazing smile. Loves to dress up and wear heels."

Well, what good will John built up, Kyle took and stomped on.

Here's what I took from his idea of a dream girl.

She needs to be smart

She needs to put his needs before his

She needs to be good looking

He worded his needs "wants" kind of harshly if you ask me. However, if you look closely, you'll notice that three ungettable qualities dominate his wish list.

The need for his dream girl to be smart is rounded up nicely in the intelligence quality.

Though an intelligent girl probably won't go for this shallow dweeb.

That's my own opinion, so allow me to carry on.

Him wanting his dream girl to put his needs before hers is covered pretty nicely in the nurture quality.

Finally, the good looking quality is covered within the sexy quality.

As I said, Kyle could have worded his needs a bit better, but they are technically within the Ungettable Purview.

MAN #5 • JOHN (A DIFFERENT ONE)

"My dream girl is a woman that is devoted, loyal, understanding, caring, and not boring... I'm an easy guy to get along with. I want a women who is spontaneous and pretty much cool with doing things that I like, well, things we both like. I want a women that doesn't mind staying in and cuddling watching a movie. Must like football!"

What I find fascinating is that sometimes, you'll read these write-ups from men and see very clearly many Ungettable qualities included.

Other times you'll read and see that they will write hundreds of words to describe one ungettable quality.

John's dream girl wish list is kind of like that.

It's a ballad to stability and mystery.

He wants someone caring, understanding, devoted, loyal, BUT NOT BORING, which is kind of ironic because what I've found is that someone who is only caring, understanding, and loyal becomes boring.

He seems to recognize this.

He wants someone spontaneous, which falls under that mystery aspect.

After explaining that he wants that adventurous girl, he does a complete 180 and talks about the need to Netflix and chill, which is the exact opposite of being spontaneous.

What he wants is someone who can provide both stability and mystery in a relationship.

MAN #6 • ANONYMOUS

"Open to talking about everything. Willing to discuss, because shit is going to happen. Willing to work through it."

Ah, this is a man I can respect.

Maybe there is hope as this man, like John before he doesn't talk about looks.

Instead, he talks about something that every lasting relationship will need.

Good communication.

So, which ungettable quality is that?

Intelligence.

I want you to go back and read that entire chapter.

If you pay attention to what it's all about is communication.

By improving or seeking to enhance your intelligence, you bring more to the table during communication.

Everything else should fall into place.

WHAT'S THE POINT OF THIS EXERCISE?

I didn't always use to do this, but now, when I take on a personal client, I make a point to explain the 12 ungettable concepts to them.

Inevitably they ask me one question.

What is the most essential quality?

It's not that they are lazy and want to focus on one concept.

It's the opposite, in fact.

They want to get results faster, so they are willing to put all of their energy into the most important quality so they can get those results quicker.

Here's the problem with that line of thinking.

Beauty is in the eye of the beholder.

What one man will find attractive another man will scoff at.

Think of it like this.

There are twelve ungettable qualities.

If you were to line one hundred men up, explain the qualities to them, and then ask them to order the qualities in order of importance, you would probably get hundreds of different orders.

Each man weighs the qualities differently.

So, spending time to master one quality isn't going to do you any good.

At the same time, it's not realistic to try to master all the qualities.

You don't have enough time and energy for that.

Instead, I think you should spend your time mastering the ones YOU feel are necessary.

You bought this book to learn how to be more attractive to men.

Whether that's some guy, you found attractive at work or an ex-boyfriend, it doesn't matter.

What annoys me is this belief that everything has to be on his terms.

You don't have to do everything for him.

Sun Tzu famously said,

"Know thyself, know thy enemy, a thousand battles, a thousand victories."

Most people gloss over a quote like that, but I don't.

Think about it for a moment.

Know thyself, know thy enemy.

Meaning that if you know yourself and you know your enemy, it will lead to success.

You can fight in a thousand battles and win every single one.

It's ok to do things for yourself.

It's ok to be selfish and pick a few ungettable qualities that you want to master for yourself as opposed to for him.

I find that the ungettable qualities have that yin and yang relationship that the holy trinity does.

Practicing one quality will have a positive effect on others.

Part Six

Self Regulation

"Empty your mind, be formless, shapeless – like water. Now you put water into a cup, it becomes the cup, you put water into a bottle, it becomes the bottle, you put it in a teapot, it becomes the teapot. Now water can flow or it can crash. Be water, my friend."

-Bruce Lee

Seventeen

Spinning Out of Control

The term "Sweet Spot" stemmed from baseball as a metaphor for the thickest part of a baseball bat.

Essentially, if the batter manages to hit the ball with the widest part of the bat, it gives him the most power, and he can control where the ball goes.

That is why a good batter can point out where he is going to send the ball before he even hits it.

So far, this book has been focused on one goal.

Showing you how to attract the right type of man.

But even after reading everything you've read and learning everything you've learned, things aren't going to go your way.

We don't live in a perfect world, and perhaps that's the most challenging thing for people.

Even if you are ungettable, not everyone will react the way you want them to.

It's easy to let this fact discourage you.

After all, one of the hardest things to deal with after heartbreak or disappointment is the feeling that your life is spinning out of control.

So, how do you deal with these unforeseen circumstances?

Self-Regulation is how you find that Sweet Spot and gain power and control over the outcome.

If you didn't know, another word for regulated is maintained.

So, when you hear me say Self-Regulated, I want you to think self-maintained.

But what are you supposed to maintain?

Well, life is a constant struggle for balance.

But life is made up of several categories.

If you focus on one area more than the others, you throw off the balance if you focus solely on things outside of you; like other people, you neglect the most crucial part of this entire equation, yourself.

> *In my opinion, the most important thing for you to master is self-discipline.*

I know.

That's not what you want to hear.

It is human nature to think you can change someone's mind by merely focusing on them.

But, that's not how being ungettable works. We focus on you and what you have control over, not on what you wish you had control over.

Here's the thing about focusing on yourself and your own goals. The closer you get to your goals, the harder it will be for most men to NOT pay attention to you.

It's uncanny how often I've seen this exact phenomenon with my breakup clients.

I suppose it all boils down to the fact that nothing stirs up doubt about whether letting a woman go was the right thing to do more than having an Ex see that you are thriving without them.

And I know that some days with my breakup clients' sadness will hit them in waves and getting out of bed seems like doing the impossible.

It's like it knocks the wind right out of them.

And yet those are the days I have to remind them that there is a light at the end of the tunnel.

That even though it's hard right now, it won't be hard forever.

The downside about dealing with the swells of sadness that will inevitably come, if they haven't already, is that the subconscious mind will try to fix itself without you even realizing it.

It will search for other sources of Dopamine and Serotonin.

That means that you might find yourself dealing with impulses to indulge in what they call a "quick fix."

- Food
- Alcohol
- Drugs
- Meaningless Sex
- Netflix
- Partying

Essentially, these are all distractions. They make you feel good for a moment, but don't lead to that Ultimate Goal of being ungettable.

This is what I mean when I talk about being self-disciplined.

You have to be able to discipline yourself and set aside what might feel good at the moment to get to what you want long-term.

When you are tempted to indulge, ask yourself, "Is this more important than working to be ungettable?"

This isn't something that happens overnight.

If you aren't already prone to Self Regulating, you can get better at it by building small habits, like setting up a schedule that you stick to and being consistent with it.

You also do it by recognizing what your stressors are and how they can cause Spirals.

Eighteen

Avoiding The Downward Spiral

Downward Spirals happen when emotions get out of control.

I always imagine overwhelming emotions as a downward track with a large funnel at the top.

No matter whether the emotions are positive or negative, they are left to follow the downward trajectory without an effort to redirect it.

Apathy is often a precursor to these downward spirals, and neutral emotions usually cause apathy.

Neutral emotions come from feeling stuck or as if you don't have control.

It's called complacency, or a general lack of interest in taking action.

This loss of motivation and the inability to set or achieve goals creates a slower downward spiral, but a downward spiral none-the-less.

It often manifests in the feeling of having lost yourself and not having direction.

When left unmanaged, it can turn into full-blown depression, which is not what we want.

When you put effort into managing your emotions, even in states of overwhelm, you can redirect them and start an Upward Spiral.

Like a roller coaster, a significant drop can be used to gain momentum and give the car enough power to start into an upward spiral.

Like we talked about a few chapters ago with momentum, all you have to do is get started.

A lot of the overwhelming emotions that you will encounter will turn out to be overthinking.

That is part of your brain's attempt to protect you.

It searches out every possible negative outcome and keeps your mind consumed with thinking up every single bad outcome.

One of my Editors has a tactic for dealing with this. In situations where we cannot possibly know the outcome, and she finds herself consumed with worry, she figures out what the absolute worst outcome is.

She calls this, "Beating em to the Punch."

Essentially, by deciding how she is going to handle the absolute worst outcome, she is already prepared to handle anything else that could happen.

Then she gets it out of her head by writing everything down in a journal.

Once your brain realizes it can handle the situation and at it's absolute worst, and it's been stored somewhere outside of your head, it will stop dwelling on it and let you turn your focus elsewhere, although there are other ways to handle Irrational Thinking.

For example, the thought "I can't live without my Ex!" is one I hear a lot from my breakup clients.

Obviously, you can live without your Ex. You lived your entire life up until the point that you met him. And your life hasn't actually ended even if it feels like it.

So, let's talk about another way you can deal with turning away the irrational thoughts your mind throws at you.

Nineteen

Overcoming Irrational Thinking

We've all been there. Your brain tries to convince you of something that would make absolutely no sense if you weren't upset.

The ways our minds do this are called Cognitive Distortions, basically an exaggerated or irrational thought pattern.

There are 15 different types of Cognitive Distortions that your mind can use to convince you of these untruths, but today we are only going to talk about one, the most common irrational belief I see in my work.

And we are going to touch on how to turn those irrational untruths into rational truths.

Without a doubt, the best "tactic" I've ever come across to help you do this is called "the rational restructure."

Think of it like this.

> *When your mind tells you something that you know on the inside isn't true, you need to find a way to restructure that thought, so it becomes your new reality.*

One of the most common irrational fears I help my clients work through is the idea that they can't handle whatever it is they are going through, whether that is a horrible breakup or being fired at work.

The pain creates this irrational fear, and the mind convinces the body that it can't handle whatever it is going through.

This is why we often see physical reactions to emotional states.

Throughout this entire book, I've been talking about the idea of the paradigm shift.

Looking at life from a different perspective and that's essentially what "the rational restructure" is.

Here's how it works.

Every time you tell yourself something like "I can't survive this."

You need to identify the false belief and reform it into a new one.

Something like,

"This hurts like hell, but I know I can handle it."

It's not magic, and it won't work overnight, but what we are looking for is momentum.

The more you force yourself to identify the false beliefs and reform them into new ones, you'll actually believe in the new reality you're creating for yourself.

Twenty

Mind Like Water

It may seem like Emotional Intelligence, and Mindset are small things to focus on in the grand scheme of things.

But, being able to react appropriately to anything that comes up along the way is paramount.

It all boils down to a straightforward concept, and we are borrowing it from a Japanese metaphor commonly referred to in martial arts as "Mizu no Kokoro", or "Mind Like Water."

The concept refers to a person's ability to calm their mind.

Zen-masters like Bruce Lee took this term to mean that

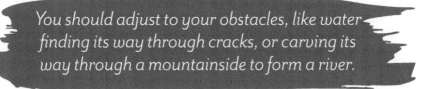

You should adjust to your obstacles, like water finding its way through cracks, or carving its way through a mountainside to form a river.

Essentially, if you are malleable, you'll find a way through.

Whereas, time-management specialist David Allen considered it in terms of how it responds and likened it to throwing a pebble into a still pond.

He asked, "How does the water respond?" and the answer he gave is just so clear and concise that I can't even begin to phrase it better.

"The water responds totally appropriately to the force and mass of the input; then it returns to calm. It doesn't overreact or underreact."

In a way, both ways of looking at it are useful. But if you don't grasp the information laid out in this book, then you will respond to pebble sized obstacles with tidal waves because you are reacting emotionally and not rationally.

So, as you can imagine, overreacting or under-reacting can seriously throw a wrench in whether you are ungettable or not.

So, say it with me,

Mind like water.

Memorize it.

Write it down.

Put it on sticky notes where you can see it often.

And, most importantly, when you are faced with something that makes you emotional and you recognize that you might respond with too much force tell yourself, "mind like water."

Part Seven

The Constant Struggle for Perfetion

"When you encounter failures and difficulties, it is vital that you boldly and joyously keep moving forward."

-The Way of The Samurai

Twenty One

Why We Procrastinate

In the case of ungettable, the actionable items I give you in the book are asking you to go against every instinct you have naturally.

Now, procrastination generally stems from the desire to do anything that's more enjoyable than the task at hand, even if we know that the outcome won't be anywhere close to what we want.

You are choosing pleasure now over a final outcome.

Think of it this way. Do you ever come face to face with those moments when you chose Netflix and the couch over putting away laundry or going to the gym?

In the same way, you are making a choice when you put off starting something today because you'd just rather not.

You get that quick hit of Dopamine from whatever you're distracting yourself with, but you are lowering your chances of becoming ungettable in the long run.

I mean, come on. You can put off doing laundry for a couple of weeks, and things will be fine. But if you don't take action in your life and change your paradigm, you definitely won't come out the other end of this on top.

How do I know? Because I see it happen EVERY SINGLE DAY!

And I don't tell you this to discourage you. I am telling you this to encourage you. You have the unique opportunity to recognize the urge to procrastinate and fight it.

And you can, no matter how difficult that choice is, and in this case, you have a large support group to push you when you have trouble pushing yourself with all the other readers of this book.

If only we had that kind of support when it came to laundry!

The Top Reasons People Aren't Ungettable

I've been coaching people for almost a decade, and I can instantly spot someone who is going to be successful versus someone who isn't.

Overall the unsuccessful exhibit four distinct qualities.

UNSUCCESSFUL QUALITY #1 • **FEAR**

Knowledge is power. But, knowing is only half of the battle past that you have to be willing to take action.

And half of the time, when you find yourself held back by fear, that fear is actually of what you DO NOT know.

I get that.

It is better to turn your focus toward what you DO know to move forward.

UNSUCCESSFUL QUALITY #2 • **IMPOSTER SYNDROME**

Feeling out of your element can put you in a state of constant "not knowing." It leaves you feeling like a fraud.

It gets you caught up between seeking perfection and puts you in a state of "not knowing" AND the fear of being found out as an imposter.

You feel like you don't deserve it, and it holds you back. Accept that you're wrong.

UNSUCCESSFUL QUALITY #3 • GETTING STARTED

Simply not knowing where to start can freeze you in your tracks.

The best way to get started is to break it down into smaller tasks until a clear starting point becomes apparent.

UNSUCCESSFUL QUALITY #4 • DISTRACTIONS

This is pretty self-explanatory, except, in the case of becoming ungettable, distractions are only more enjoyable than putting in the effort to move forward to an end that isn't promised.

Twenty Three

How Do You Overcome Procrastination?

Turn your focus from short-term to long-term.

This doesn't mean that you can't enjoy the present moment. You should still enjoy the present but consider the trade-off.

How important is becoming ungettable to you?

Is it worth momentarily doing something that may not exactly be fun?

Plan things out in advance. When you come across actionable items, commit yourself.

Put it on the calendar.

Schedule it.

Don't rely on will power to get you moving.

Say "No.' to overload. Don't let people or things waste your time.

Obtaining ungettable status is about becoming the best version of yourself. And the best part about that is that you get to define what that is.

Don't allow things into your life that don't serve that vision.

Be deliberate and have a sense of urgency.

Think about the last time you procrastinated on something. How much did you accomplish during the time that you were working?

Think about how much you could get done if you had that sense of urgency the whole time you have available.

Somehow, in that state, I have seen people do incredible things.

You can do far more than you think you can.

Opt for progress and excellence, not perfection. Perfection is an impossible goal.

Most of the time, when someone sets a goal to be perfect, they are merely making sure that there isn't a solid finish line.

It is just another way to put things off; this also applies to waiting for the 'right time" or the "right circumstances."

You are setting an impossible end goal.

Right now is probably the most uncertain you've felt about anything in a long time. And I get it.

Literally, everyone you talk to has an opinion about how you should handle your situation. Every "coach" that works in this niche tries to sell you on a guarantee that they can make any man fall for you.

And you can't seem to get any information on what men are thinking, doing, or why they're doing it.

I mean, you've taken the first step by buying this book, but I've showered you with knowledge that you might not know how to act on yet.

It's information overload with absolutely none of the information you want or think you need. Not to mention, the sheer overwhelm of what you are feeling can keep most of you frozen in fear because it is easier to wait for the "right moment" to take action than actually to take action.

Meanwhile, there's always someone else out there working on getting that ungettable status. To steal the one man that might be right for you for the rest of your life.

I'm not here to try to explain men's actions.

I've tried that in the past, and it doesn't add any value to the effort to make you ungettable. It only serves as a distraction from what you should be doing.

Go figure.

So, let's start with a hard truth.

Did you know that 92% of people who set goals never actually reach them?

I don't say that to discourage you. I say that so that we can focus on something that makes that other 8% successful.

So many people come into expecting other people to do the work for them.

And they couldn't be more wrong.

This book gives you plenty of things to do to start your journey towards becoming an ungettable girl, and they aren't just to pass the time.

They are things that get results.

But the trick is, you have to take action on them to be successful.

Our goal here is to beat the odds. I want this book to be the one that takes that statistic and turns it on its head.

I want every single one of you to succeed and overcome procrastination.

That's right.

I want 100% of you to succeed.

Nine times out of ten, the things that happen in your life are your responsibility.

It's so easy to get stuck in a victim mindset and pretend like everything happens to us.

I'm right there with you.

Don't let yourself make excuses.

Accept responsibility and OWN IT today... Not tomorrow.

Here's the thing.

Tomorrow-you is not your friend.

The things you couldn't bring yourself to do today aren't going to be fun or easy to do tomorrow magically.

And while there will be days that it is easier, there is no guarantee that tomorrow will be that day.

It's easy to believe that tomorrow is going to be the day that everything falls into place and that tomorrow-you is going to wake up competent, capable, and ready to face the day.

But guess what!

You are going to go to bed with it being today and looking forward to tomorrow.

And the only magic that is going to happen is that when you wake up, tomorrow has become today.

It keeps getting pushed forward.

So, there are only two ways to get things done.

You should start working towards your goals as soon as possible.

So, that means you start now or create a plan now.

Anything that requires a plan should be broken down into steps or Milestones.

The first actionable step is called the Next Action.

If there is one thing, I can tell you it's to stop waiting for circumstances to be perfect to work towards a goal.

As anyone can tell you, even in the best moments, circumstances aren't perfect.

Procrastination becomes a habit. Break the habit today. Don't put that off until tomorrow, either.

None of this is to discourage you. It's to encourage you. It's to tell you what is possible if you don't put things off till tomorrow.

In this book, when you define a goal or a Next Action if your first instinct is to put it off, don't.

You can't reach the finish line if you don't run the race.

So, take the first step. Run the race.

Twenty Four

The Struggle for Perfection

It is human nature to seek the unobtainable.

The one prevailing question that I wanted to answer when I started writing this book was,

"How can you become the one thing every man wants, but no man can touch?"

These are the kind of thoughts that keep me up at night.

Odd, right?

I've often been called a perfectionist by those who know me.

I suppose you could say it's my fatal flaw. About six months ago, I had to get pretty major surgery.

I won't bore you with the details because this book is about you more than it is about me.

But I will say this.

I asked so many questions to the recovery nurses when I woke up that her first response was,

"You're a perfectionist, aren't you?"

Here's the thing about perfection.

It truly is unobtainable.

No matter how hard you try to be ungettable, you're bound to fail in some way or hit some roadblock that prevents you from succeeding.

These are the times you will truly be tested.

You'll be down on yourself.

Your subconscious will make you believe the lies you've always thought about yourself.

That you're not good enough.

That you can't possibly become this "ungettable" person.

Most people, when faced with any kind of adversity, will give up because it's too damn hard to push through the pain and persevere.

This may sound insensitive, but I have no sympathy for quitters.

I never have, and I never will.

I can't tell you how often I've put my own time and energy into helping women over the years only to have them give up before they saw any kind of results.

The funny part is that I get blamed because I didn't help them or solve their problems when the reality is that they simply quit.

Blaming me is easier than blaming themselves.

Did they quit because of fear?

Was it too hard?

Were they too emotionally unstable after a breakup to execute properly?

Maybe.

This politically correct culture wants me to Shepard the quitters.

No man or woman left behind, they say.

Apparently, they aren't students of history.

Men and women have always been left behind.

Maybe this is an overly simplistic view, but I believe there are two types of people in the world.

The wolves and the sheep.

Which are you?

Wolves lead, and sheep follow.

Some will have you believe that you are either born a wolf or a sheep.

I don't think that's true.

I think your environment has a lot to do with what you think you are.

If you surround yourself by sheep and all you hear your entire life is that you are a sheep eventually, it just becomes this universal truth, you believe.

But it doesn't have to be.

In every soul, there is a will to lead.

There is a wolf.

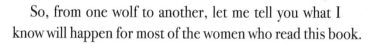

So, from one wolf to another, let me tell you what I know will happen for most of the women who read this book.

They'll probably like it.

If I'm personally lucky, they'll hop on Amazon to give it a good review.

Which by the way, I hate breaking the fourth wall like this but please do that if you haven't already.

Maybe if they're lucky, my words will stay with them for a few days.

But like all things, the words will fade.

They'll tell themselves that they'll take action and maybe they will.

They'll take out a sheet of paper and jot a few of the best ideas down.

They'll seek to be ungettable.

For a few weeks, they'll do just the things they think are important, and they probably won't see much of a change.

That small negative will turn into a big negative as they altogether quit and move on with their lives.

I only know that this happens because this is exactly what happens to me when I get fired up after reading something interesting.

I'll tell myself,

"I'm doing this right away."

And I will.

But I don't keep up with it.

Life gets in the way and like I said, my fatal flaw is perfectionism.

So, when perfectionism doesn't immediately come, I tend to give up.

It wasn't until I stumbled across the way of the samurai that I truly understood.

Perhaps the most profound paradigm shift I took from reading about the ancient Samurai was how they viewed perfection.

"One should spend their whole lifetime diligently learning as much as they can. In this way you will become a more developed and fully realized human being with each passing day. The goal of total perfection has no end."

It's that last part that particularly struck me.

The goal of total perfection has no end.

They would live their entire lives, understanding that perfection is impossible.

But that doesn't mean that you shouldn't seek to attain it. The journey of doing so is what shapes and molds you into an impressive individual.

Trying to become ungettable is a little like that.

It might very well be impossible to obtain, but one thing is sure, if you never try to capture it, you won't experience the amazing results of the journey.

Being ungettable is just a symptom of an endless pursuit of perfection.

Nothing more, nothing less.

Made in the USA
Columbia, SC
21 October 2023